DISASTER RECOVERY PLANNING FOR NONPROFITS

Michael K. Robinson

LSTA-04-0103-1108   "Funding for this grant was awarded by the Illinois State Library (ISL), a division of the Office of Secretary of State, using funds provided by the Institute of Museum and Library Services (IMLS), under the federal Library Services and Technology Act (LSTA)."

Hamilton Books

an imprint of
University Press of America,® Inc.
Dallas · Lanham · Boulder · New York · Oxford

Copyright © 2003 by
Hamilton Books
4501 Forbes Boulevard
Suite 200
Lanham, Maryland 20706
UPA Acquisitions Department (301) 459-3366

PO Box 317
Oxford
OX2 9RU, UK

Library of Congress Control Number: 2003111419
ISBN 0-7618-2660-2 (paperback : alk. ppr.)

Contents

Preface

Nonprofits have never considered themselves to be part of a normal industry. They have always separated themselves by at least an arm's length from their commercial counterparts. Maybe it is because of their goals and mission statements, which are very different than those of for-profit companies. Maybe it is because they often have less unrestricted income or because their employees are dedicated to the cause of the organization. It is difficult to pinpoint, but something about their very nature is fundamentally different.

The public has come to expect more from nonprofits than they do from other organizations. The public demands fiscal accountability, sound management practices, zero tolerance for scandal, and top-notch efficiency. The public has a perception and in some instances the expectation that nonprofits are poor and are to have nearly every dollar go directly to program services. It is an amazing double standard. How are nonprofits to thrive? There is public and media outcry when nonprofit CEOs are well compensated, yet the public wants excellent management. People have higher expectations of nonprofits than they do of commercial organizations and even the government. If the cost to fundraising ratio for a nonprofit is above the arbitrary number set by watchdog groups such as the Better Business Bureau, the nonprofit gets blacklisted. The government and state conducted lotteries do not have the same scrutiny. Commercial organizations are not expected to have the same efficiency, although stockholders do have certain demands. Not only is there something different about nonprofits, the public insists on it.

On the flip side, the public feels for nonprofits. There is something sad or something a little disturbing when there is news of a charity or nonprofit that must close its doors. It is more upsetting to hear that a nonprofit has to stop its philanthropic efforts – when the Good Samaritan announces he can no longer aid those in need. This becomes even more heart wrenching when it is a result of a disaster (a disaster being any number of incidents, such as fire, flood, theft, scandal, computer failure, etc.). It is as if the will to continue to help is still present but the physical means to do so are gone. It is similar to the phrase, "the mind is willing but the body is not able." It strikes a devastating chord to realize that not only are employees without jobs, but that the recipients of the nonprofit's works will need to do without. These people will be required to find other resources to meet their needs. Whether the effect is on the local community level, such as a soup kitchen closing its doors, or on the national level such as a cancer related organization no longer funding treatment and research – it is sad. A bit of us disappears, too. Nonprofits need to address the issue of sound management practices concerning disaster recovery planning to keep their hopes and efforts alive.

Disaster recovery planning is not new. Nonprofits just have not adopted implementation of it. It could be because planning is not directly tied to a program or service of the organization, the nonprofit does not know how to implement a plan, or the employees just do not have the time. It is difficult to say what exactly the reason is. It probably differs from organization to organization. It is also true that nonprofits are not driven by technology, but technology is not the only element of a plan. Whatever the reason, nonprofits need to shift their focus.

A spring 2003 survey showed that only 46% of the responding nonprofits had a disaster recovery plan in place. The survey also showed that many of the existing plans were inadequate. While 46% might not sound too egregious, it is very likely that this number is higher than the true statistical average of the industry. Over 400 nonprofits were invited by e-mail to participate in the online survey, yet only 10% did. Several organizations anonymously confessed that they did not want to publicly admit that they did not have a plan in place. Many invitees simply chose not to respond in any way. According to the AAFRC Trust for Philanthropy, the IRS has stated that there are over 865,000 registered charities in the United States and that number does not include churches and grass roots organizations (2002). Obtaining an accurate gauge of the current practices may be difficult; however this survey does paint an informative picture about the current trends of nonprofits. Comparison to another statistic may place the nonprofit survey in perspective. A recent statistic stated that of all commercial organizations, a sector which is often ahead of nonprofits in terms of implementing new policies, business practices, and technology, only 10% have implemented a disaster recovery plan.

While the spring 2003 survey of nonprofits may not indicate the practices of the entire industry, it does identify some interesting trends. (The survey's results appear in Appendix A – Nonprofit Survey Results.) The conclusions indicate that many nonprofits are not prepared to handle a disaster. While those nonprofits with plans are better equipped to deal with a disaster than their non-plan implementing counterparts, they, too, are not as prepared as they should be and may have a sense of false security. Clearly something needs to be done about how nonprofits address disaster recovery planning. This book is aimed towards providing nonprofits with the knowledge and ability to begin the implementation of a comprehensive strategy. For those with plans already in place, it will serve as an aid in auditing their current practices.

After reading this text, some readers may be surprised in two ways. First, the use of technology, while important to disaster recovery planning efforts, does not take center stage and is not the primary focus of the book. As it will be explained, this is because many aspects of a plan for nonprofits will include other areas – areas which are often overlooked. Second, the book is not very long. There are many details in plan implementation and these details will vary from organization to organization as plans take shape based on budget, manpower, and additional resources. Many nonprofits will have unique needs. A nonprofit will need to create and devise its own plan rather than copy a standard format. This text lays the framework for plan development. Additionally, some of the subject areas covered in the text, especially those surrounding technology, can be elaborated on at great length, which in turn may bog down non-technical staff. The purpose here is to provide a sound and comprehensive overview for creating and implementing a strategy. Details and supporting information are included as necessary. The technology and methods used to develop disaster recovery practices will continue to change and evolve into tools which will make implementation easier. The overall approach to developing plans and practices will be able to remain in tact.

Creating a good disaster recovery plan is not easy. It will require the active support and endorsement of top management down to lower level employees and possibly volunteers. While nonprofits are different than their counterparts, it is true that they have internal and external politics just as their corporate brethren. If this first hurdle can be overcome, a nonprofit has the ability to make significant strides in its planning efforts and implementation. Nonprofits will need to adopt and integrate these strategies if the organizations hope to meet the public's need and become long lasting influences.

Michael Robinson
Crofton, MD
May 30, 2003

Chapter 1
Introducing Nonprofits to Disaster Recovery

Disaster recovery planning, while not an entirely new concept, has gained increased attention since the events of 9/11 and the formation of the Department of Homeland Security. The topic however, has not become well rooted in the nonprofit community. Nonprofits do not seem to be intentional targets of disasters or more vulnerable than their commercial counterparts, but they are not less susceptible to these types of occurrence either. A disaster can take the shape of events other than a terrorist attack. The occurrence could be a natural phenomenon such as a fire, flood, earthquake, heavy snow, or tornado. It could be the result of faulty equipment, such as data loss, interrupted utility service (gas, electricity, telephone, or Internet connection), or computer network malfunction. It may be an issue related to the human operational side of the nonprofit, such as the loss of key personnel, a work related accident, theft of files or equipment, or even a dreaded financial scandal. Disasters can take many forms and can vary in size from minor incident to major catastrophe. An efficient disaster recovery plan should be designed to protect the entire nonprofit – its employees, systems, and information – in the event of any major disaster (therefore covering minor incidents as well) so the organization may resume its philanthropic activities as quickly as possible. It appears that nonprofits have not developed disaster recovery plans as quickly as their government or commercial counterparts. The initial

Case History:
Preparing For the Un-
thinkable

On September 11, 2001,
Helen Keller Worldwide
was destroyed by the
debris from the World
Trade Center. The cost to
rebuild was in excess of
4 million dollars. In
addition to all records
and databases being de-
stroyed (and still being
rebuilt to this day), the
archives of Helen Keller
were destroyed. The only
item salvaged was a bust
of Helen Keller.

fear of dealing with disaster recovery, feelings that a disaster will not happen to them, or a lack of understanding of the issues are the most likely reasons why nonprofits may not be prepared. However, the threat of a disaster hindering or halting the work of nonprofits is very real and until it receives open admission and is adequately addressed, nonprofits are at risk.

Getting Beyond the Initial Fear

People, in general, seem to have an aversion to disaster recovery planning. It is not the planning part that creates the roadblock, but rather they get hung up on the thought of a disaster. As individuals we do not like the thought of surrendering control during an impossible situation. As a group we do not like the concept of our framework (the nonprofit, the place of employment, etc.) becoming disrupted. Nonprofits might be especially prone to these aversions. Some nonprofits and charitable organizations have been formed to provide assistance to the community. Many organizations, such as the American Red Cross, CARE, and Catholic Relief Services provide relief services to communities in severe or disastrous situations. But when it comes time to address the possibility of being victims themselves, nonprofits become proverbial ostriches with their heads in the sand. In a spring 2003 nonprofit survey only 48% of respondents indicated they had a disaster recovery plan in place at the time of the survey. This number does not seem too promising, and upon further inspection it was revealed that the picture does not get better. The same survey identified the following (Additional results appear in Appendix A – Nonprofit Survey.):

- 69% of the respondents made an effort to back up the essential legal documents, such as tax-exempt applications,

990s, audits, and insurance policies, but only 55% of those organizations backed up all of the necessary documents.

- 59% of those who back up their essential legal documents store copies of those documents off-site.
- 52% of all respondents store their tapes and paper documents in fire-proof safes or cabinets, but 73% of those organizations do not know if their fire-proof containers are rated for paper or electronic media.
- 93% of all respondents have recorded the home phone numbers of employees, but only 76% of all respondents have identified a contact person to notify for each employee in the event of an employee accident. Only 54% of those who store these numbers have the lists available off-site.
- 50% of those with disaster recovery plans have conducted an analysis in an attempt to identify risks or threats to the organization.
- 24% of those with a disaster recovery plan had incorporated the use of an emergency site, such as a hot site, cold site, or mobile site in their plan.
- 45% of those with disaster recovery plans have tested their plans.
- 45% of all respondents have conducted fire drills.

It is clear that while a nonprofit may have a disaster recovery plan in place, it is likely it is inadequate. Nonprofits need to address the challenges of forming effective disaster recovery plans if they are to continue in their roles of serving the community.

Individuals form contingency plans for themselves all the time. Let's get personal: do you have health insurance? Dental insurance? Car insurance? Life insurance? Short- or long-term disability insurance? A will? And more importantly, *why* do you have any of these? Do you carry them because the prospect of not having them could become so expensive that it is frightening and could lead to bankruptcy? Maybe you want a guarantee that your family will receive provisions should an accident or something worse occur? Maybe it is just the peace of mind in knowing that the safeguard is there. Nonprofits should not manage their organizations any differently. A disaster recovery plan places emphasis on forming a type of contingency plan – one designed to help a nonprofit resume normal or near-normal activities after a disaster strikes. It does not mean the nonprofit is looking for its own demise or impending doom, but rather is looking forward to its longevity. Self-preservation is an underlying principle in a nonprofit's mission. They can not help others if they are not in a position to function.

Is the Need For a Disaster Recovery Plan Real?

Disaster recovery planning is not a luxury for nonprofit organizations – it is essential. Nonprofits do not have large reserves to carry themselves through difficult situations. Often funds are limited and resources are scarce. A devastating event could wipe out any existing budget. The B&O Railroad Museum experienced such a situation. The museum, located in Baltimore, Maryland, was the victim of a disaster in February 2003 when its roof collapsed under the weight of heavy snow. Several irreplaceable exhibits were damaged or destroyed. The six year's worth of repairs are estimated at around twenty million dollars, and it is unlikely that insurance will cover all expenses. This museum experienced a terrible setback. A gala fundraising event to be held at the facility in two weeks' time had to be cancelled. If a similar tragedy were to strike the home office of your nonprofit, would it survive? Providing adequate protection for a nonprofit to deal with such an occurrence will take both time and money to implement but is worth it. Also weighing on the minds of nonprofit leaders is the increasing pressure of financial accountability. Necessary equipment, such as tape drives (and a good supply of tapes) is often at the bottom of expenditure lists. The need for creating a plan is all too real, but its actual development often falls to the wayside. Nonprofits cannot afford to hide from disaster recovery planning.

According to statistics released by Security Education Systems in January 2002, 50% of a community's businesses would be out of business if a disaster were to strike the region. The same statistics claimed that only 10% of the nation's businesses have developed an effective disaster recovery plan (Turner, 2002). This does not bode well for the nonprofit sector, which typically lags behind its corporate counterparts in implementing new strategies.

In disaster recovery measures it appears that time is of the essence. IBM conducted post-disaster research that specified that certain industries needed to be up and running within a given amount of time, e.g., finance: 2 days, commerce: 3.5 days, industrial: 5 days, insurance: 5.5 days. Of the companies whose systems were not operational within the time limits given:

- 25% went bankrupt immediately
- 40% closed their doors within the next two years
- Of the 35% remaining, nearly none were around five years after the disaster (Tagger, 2002).

Not only is it important to have a disaster recovery plan in place, it needs to be both effective and quick to implement. Gaining knowledge about how a disaster will affect a nonprofit, how long it will take to restore systems, and how it will impact employees is essential.

The Basic Cycle of Events in Disaster and Recovery

Before rushing off to form a plan, it is important to understand the various phases that occur from the time a disaster hits to the time that normal operations resume. Each phase has unique characteristics although the length of each will vary from disaster to disaster. A good disaster recovery plan will address each phase of the recovery process and recognize that not every part of the nonprofit can be restored instantly. The basic elements in the timeline of events include the actual disaster, the immediate response, short-term recovery, long-term recovery, and resumption. A graphical depiction of this timeline appears in Figure 1.1. The disaster recovery plan itself includes all activities from immediate response to resumption. Not all levels of the response will require the same level of decision-making and activity. People tend to react to a disaster first and then begin to think and rationalize as recovery procedures takes place. It is human nature. An effective plan will take this into consideration. Through efficient planning and training, people will respond more efficiently and with less panicked minds during an emergency. As the nonprofit moves further away from the disaster and more towards resumption, more active thinking will be performed. A brief description of each step of the timeline follows:

Disaster

A disaster is an event that interrupts one or more functions of the nonprofit. They may vary in severity. A catastrophic disaster is one where all operations at the nonprofit cease. Minor disasters may be ones where only one or two departments are disrupted. The type of disaster will determine the appropriate course of action.

Immediate response

The immediate response is the first reaction to the disaster once it has been identified. It may sound odd to mention identification, but not all disasters are of the same magnitude and some may be slow to spot. A building fire is relatively easy to identify, but a flood that occurs in a rarely visited basement may go unnoticed for some time.

Short-term recovery

The recovery steps that bring all essential systems on-line after the immediate response are termed short-term. Short-term disaster recovery typically takes between 2-6 days for major crises. The longer the delay in successfully completing a short-term recovery the more likely it is the nonprofit organization will never recover from the disaster.

Long-term recovery

After all essential systems have been restored, important systems are then re-initiated. This step in the recovery process may take longer to complete than short-term recovery plans. The functions restored at this stage of the recovery are relevant to the day-to-day operations of the nonprofit, but they are not as vital as those restored during the short-term recovery process.

Resumption

The final step in a disaster recovery plan occurs when all day-to-day activities have resumed. All essential, important, and useful systems and related events are taking place. Resumption is not necessarily the same as the normal activities that were occurring

Figure 1.1 –   *Timeline of events for a disaster and a recovery plan execution*

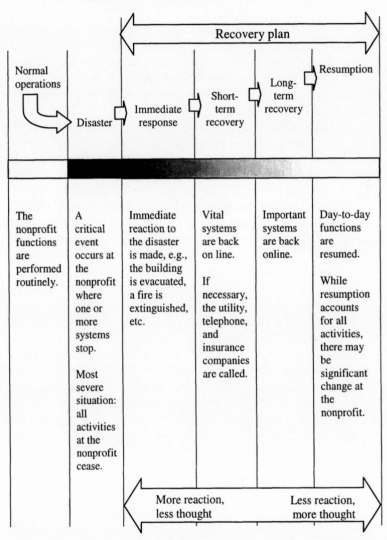

The time between the actual disaster and the time it takes to get vital systems online is critical. The longer it takes to get those key systems up and running the more likely it is that the nonprofit will not recover from the disaster. Companies that have experienced down-time greater than the typical 2-6 days usually do not survive.

prior to the disaster. The nonprofit may be located in new office space, have different equipment, and be working from scratch in some areas. Resumption means that normal or near-normal activities are taking place and the nonprofit will for the most part continue to function in this new pattern of activity. A nonprofit may try to make the most of an ill-fated situation, such as finally implementing hardware upgrades that have been long postponed or adopting new procedures.

Disaster recovery planning needs to become one of the standard business practices of nonprofits. The present safeguards employed by many nonprofits suggest that current strategies are not adequate. Nonprofits need to establish a plan to deal with all of the phases of disaster recovery. Through defining a proper disaster recovery plan, a nonprofit can focus its time and attention on the important philanthropic activities of the organization and rest a little easier knowing that if a disaster occurs, they will be prepared.

Questions for Review and Implementation

1. What types of disasters could affect a nonprofit organization?
2. What are the current trends in disaster recovery practices employed by nonprofits?
3. What are the possible reasons for nonprofits not implementing disaster recovery plans?
4. What are the major events on the timeline of disaster recovery planning?
5. Why would the normal operating practices of a nonprofit be different when it resumes its activities after a disaster?

Chapter 2
Team Formation and Initial Plan Development

A nonprofit will need to spend considerable energy and forethought in forming its disaster recovery plan. A basic assumption in its implementation is that the nonprofit has decided this is a necessary investment of resources – after all, this will not be a regular service or program of the organization and it will appear as administrative overhead. In a time when particular attention is given to scrutinizing how much of a nonprofit's revenue goes directly to programs this may be an issue. If money were no object, all nonprofits would have state of the art disaster recovery plans. Fiscal concerns will play a critical role in how developed the nonprofit's plan will become. However, even with limited financial resources, a nonprofit can develop a reasonable plan. How much time, money, and effort to expend can be decided later, but first an agreement should be reached. If the forming and implementing of a plan does not have the full support of at least key individuals (managers, directors, a few employees, and possibly the board of directors), the plan will either fall flat or continually get pushed to a back burner. Upon deciding to undertake the process, one of the first steps is forming a well-balanced team.

Disaster recovery plans cannot rest on the shoulders of one person. One individual will not have the knowledge of the entire organization's day-to-day activities and he or she may not have the necessary time to prepare documentation, perform audits, conduct risk analyses, and test a plan. If the nonprofit is so small that the process of building a disaster recovery plan needs to be undertaken by a team of one, care should be given to ensure that the plan has a balanced approach. At least some input should come from another individual. Thought should also be given to the possibility that in a disaster that one person may be injured or become unavailable to implement a recovery plan, which will render the entire plan useless.

Ideally the nonprofit should form a disaster recovery team with a leader. This team approach will allow for the nonprofit to divide up activities, allow for internal checks and balances between divisions, and ensure that the entire organization is covered in the disaster recovery plan. A team will ensure that at least one knowledgeable person will be equipped to begin executing the plan, if necessary. A team approach however is not the same as forming a committee. Committees where everything is achieved through elaborate discussions and consensus will not be effective in this situation. The end result may often become too big and too overwhelming for implementation because every committee member may feel the need to over emphasize the importance of his or her department. The team should contain enough members to identify the vital operations of the nonprofit and contribute in the plan's implementation.

A team leader should be someone who commands enough respect in the nonprofit to get things done. This individual does not need to be the head of the organization or even the head of the IT department, but he or she should be someone to whom employees will listen and respond. This leader will need to be someone who is comfortable making decisions and who has a cool head in hot situations. If the time ever comes that the disaster recovery plan will need to be executed, the team leader will be the person in charge during recovery and resumption.

The rest of the team should be formed of representatives from various departments who can identify the critical systems that are essential to the functioning of the nonprofit. No employee will be familiar with all of the day-to-day operations of all departments/aspects of the organization. This is why you need a balanced team. On some occasions it may be helpful to bring several members from one department on to the team, such as several members from the IS/IT department. Avoid bringing too many individuals from one group. This may create a lopsided disaster recovery plan with too much emphasis in one particular area while others may be under-emphasized or even ignored.

Another consideration in forming a balanced team is the administrative rights held by various individuals throughout the nonprofit. Information throughout an organization will not be accessible to all employees. For example, personnel files with salary information may be available only to individuals in the human resources department. Fundraisers might be the only ones with access to lists of donors. Administrative permissions on a network server may belong to just one or two users. The very nature of secure information and privacy will dictate that some individuals be included on the team.

Disaster recovery planning has often been relegated to the world of IT because of the need for efficient and reliable technology. Most books on the subject matter can be found in the computer section at the local bookstore. Disaster recovery planning rarely makes it to the business section and definitely not to nonprofits. While the use of computers, high-tech devices, and the Internet will play critical roles in disaster recovery planning, the entire plan development should not be turned over solely to the IT department. If it is, the plan will most likely not be complete nor will it be entirely reliable. One needs only to look at the rise and fall of the dot-coms to make a case for this argument. Good disaster recovery planning needs to be the product of effective collaboration between all departments. Once a team is in place, action items can be defined.

Moving Into High Gear

With the appropriate personnel the nonprofit can begin to form an appropriate disaster recovery plan. Each nonprofit will have a unique plan. Before marching off in a dozen different directions, the nonprofit should conduct some external and internal research in the form of audits. This will maximize the coverage of the plan while minimizing the amount of work to be done. The audits should identify every activity and function of the nonprofit organization and the steps involved in each. Audits should be conducted by various team members of all of the nonprofit's departments so the core components of the recovery plan can be identified. The core design of a nonprofit's disaster recovery plan should protect the following:

- The organization's assets
- The organization's procedures
- Information which exists in paper form
- Information which exists in electronic form

A good team leader should resist the urge to over-simplify the core design of the plan. For example, some nonprofits go to reasonable length to protect electronic data with a backup tape and provide an insurance policy to replace lost or damaged equipment while ignoring essential information that exists in paper form.

When performing an audit, disaster recovery team members should look at every aspect of the nonprofit organization. The successful approach is to outline every activity of the nonprofit and prioritize each according to its relationship to the mission of the nonprofit. The mechanism by which each activity is performed is called a system. Some activities may require the interaction of multiple systems. Each department should be consulted in this stage of plan development. The result will identify systems that can be broken down into three categories. They are:

1. Vital systems

Those systems which are absolutely necessary for the nonprofit to function are considered vital. A site's utilities can definitely be considered vital to the organization. Depending on how the nonprofit conducts business, telephone systems may be considered vital.

2. Important systems

These systems are not essential for the nonprofit to conduct business but are considered important for the nonprofit to function efficiently. E-mail capability is generally viewed as an important system. There was a time when e-mail did not exist, but it is now becoming a primary form of communication. With the way nonprofits conduct business in current times, e-mail systems are moving closer to vital system status.

3. Useful systems

Systems which are helpful to the nonprofit's functioning but are not vital or important are considered useful systems. Being able to reach the Internet to search for information is a useful system and can save time by quickly locating information, but it is generally not considered essential in day-to-day business.

Every nonprofit is going to define vital, important, and useful systems differently. An inner-city feeding program may find the ability to work kitchen appliances vital to the operations of the nonprofit, where an advocacy group which needs to issue citizen alerts will rely heavily on e-mail. Nonprofit organizations which provide general accounting services will find computer spreadsheet programs indispensable, but a small animal shelter may be able to write checks and keep ledgers by hand. The nature of the nonprofit will help determine the priority of various systems and depending upon the specific day-to-day activities of the organization, systems will receive different rankings. Once an audit has been performed by the disaster recovery team, it is time to begin protecting the organization's assets. Additional information on identifying systems is discussed in *Protecting the Organization's Activities,* which appears in the next chapter.

Protecting the Organization's Assets

Flat out: employees are a nonprofit's most valuable asset. Considerable time and effort are spent educating and training them. They conduct all the work of the nonprofit and carry out the programs. Salaries are typically the highest expense after program expenditures. The nonprofit relies on its employees for business just as employees rely on the nonprofit for employment. Many times the relationship is so symbiotic that the nonprofit assumes the character of its employees. Their identities become mixed. And this doesn't even tap into the volunteer staffs upon which so many nonprofits are dependent. It makes sense to include the protection of employees in the disaster recovery plan. (This also has the added benefit of reducing a nonprofit's liability.)

Provide employees with the basic safety information of their site. This may sound slightly absurd, but it guarantees that incorrect assumptions are corrected and that everyone has the same common knowledge. Aside from letting employees know that a disaster recovery team exists (who knows – it may even generate some enthusiastic volunteers), inform them of:

- All of the fire exits in the building
- The location of the fire alarms
- The location of fire extinguishers
- The proper place to go in the event of a building evacuation

Some of this information may seem very basic and even like common sense, but it is often overlooked. How often have you seen the nearest fire alarm to the point where you don't even notice it anymore? When is the last time your nonprofit conducted a fire drill? As children we all practiced school fire drills to the point of *ad nauseum*. This addresses the point of people reacting and not thinking during the immediate reaction stage following a disaster. Examples of well planned evacuation drills can be found in London, England. Green "Fire Assembly Point" signs can be found throughout the streets of London, which identify where building occupants should gather in the event of a fire or evacuation.

Sharing Information

Provide all existing employees and every new employee upon arrival a copy of your nonprofit's emergency information. A sample emergency information sheet appears in Figure 2.1. This sheet gives several phone numbers so any employee can contact the disaster recovery team leader and take initial action, if necessary. The emergency sheet should also list the full address of the organization in the event that the information is needed for rescue personnel. While not every employee will serve on the disaster recovery team, a lone person working after hours may need to contact the people listed in the event of an emergency.

Information between the nonprofit and the employees is a two-way street. Employees will need to share information with the nonprofit as well. Nonprofits, like most commercial organizations, will collect personnel related information for the purpose of hiring an individual. Once hired, an employee's file usually gets locked away until a performance review comes around. That information is not available to all the members of the disaster recovery team and should not be considered the general source. Nonprofits will need to collect several pieces of information about employees and that information must be accessible to at least the disaster recovery team, if not organization-wide. Data to be collected should include:

- Employee's home and/or cell phone numbers for the purposes of contacting them after hours or on the weekend. In the event that employees need to be told not to report to the normal workplace this information will be critical.

- The employee's normal work location. Employees become quite familiar with their work environments. Conveying this information to emergency personnel such as fire rescuers is critical and timing is of the essence. Emergency contact sheets can be given to emergency response personnel (along with a floor plan of the facility) to aid in search and recovery.

- A contact person to identify in the event of an

Case History:
The Value of Getting Employees On Board

In the summer of 2002 as a nonprofit attempted to begin forming a communication tree, several employees were reluctant to provide home phone numbers and the names and numbers of people to contact in the event of an emergency. After several attempts to get cooperation, the employees said they would happily provide that information at the time of the emergency or that anyone could retrieve the information from his or her personnel file. The reluctant employees were countered with the following question: "When you're knocked out and being taken to the hospital, how are you going to tell me who to call? And if I can get into your locked file, can I see how much you're paid while I'm there?" All of the employees gladly helped with the phone tree from that point forward.

accident for each em-ployee. The daytime and evening phone numbers should be available. This information is extremely important if a person should be rendered un-conscious or is transported to a medical center. It is not acceptable to think that if an employee gets hurt, he or she can be asked whom to call at that point in time. Examples employee emergency contact sheets appear in Figures 2-1 and Figure 2-2.

With the gathered information a phone tree should be established so details concerning an emergency can be communicated between employees. Having a phone tree may not seem to be an entirely complex idea but several items should be kept in mind when forming it:

- The tree should be built prior to a disaster and distributed to all employees. Deciding who will call whom during the commotion will not only increase confusion, it will guarantee that someone will be overlooked.
- All employees should be accounted for on the list. Do not assume that word will automatically get around.
- Design a closed-face tree. A closed-face tree will have a loop that will enable a confirmation that all employees have been contacted. The individual who starts the process, i.e., the disaster recovery team leader, should be notified when all employees have been reached.
- Design a wide tree with many branches rather than a long one with a few branches. Information needs to travel quickly. Having a shorter tree will enable this.
- Define a procedure for the tree to still function in the event that an individual cannot be reached. Information should continue to move down the tree even if someone is unavailable.
- Lastly, when using the tree, have employees write down the important facts which need to be passed down the chain. This is an emergency information tree, not a gossip chain. Avoid having information diluted. Writing things down will make certain that specific facts are passed along without error.

Figure 2.1 – Contact Information Sheet

Disaster Recovery Plan
Contact Information Sheet

Your nonprofit
5555 Anywhere Street, Suite 200
Anytown, MD 21114

Fire department: (____) ____-_____
Rescue/ambulance: (____) ____-_____
Police department: (____) ____-_____

Disaster Recovery Team Leader: _____
Work phone number: (____)____-_____ext. _____
Home phone number: (____) ____-_____
Cell phone number: (____) ____-_____

Gas company: (____) ____-_____ Acct.: _____
Water company: (____) ____-_____ Acct.: _____
Electric company: (____) ____-_____ Acct.: _____
Telephone company: (____) ____-_____ Acct.: _____
Alarm company: (____) ____-_____ Acct.: _____

Hot site/cold site/mobile site
Address: _____
            _____

Telephone: (____) ____-_____

Location to go to in the event of an evacuation:
_____

The internal fire alarm (does / does not) contact the fire
department.

Figure 2.2 – Employee Emergency Contact Information

Employee Emergency Contact Information

Employee's name: _____
Office location: _____
Work telephone number: (____) _____-_____
Home telephone number: (____) _____-_____
Cell phone number: (____) _____-_____

Person to notify in the event of an emergency: _____

                Work telephone number: (____) _____-_____
                Home telephone number: (____) _____-_____
                Cell phone number: (____) _____-_____

Employee Emergency Contact Information

Employee's name: _____
Office location: _____
Work telephone number: (____) _____-_____
Home telephone number: (____) _____-_____
Cell phone number: (____) _____-_____

Person to notify in the event of an emergency: _____

Work telephone number: (____) _____-_____
Home telephone number: (____) _____-_____
Cell phone number: (____) _____-_____

With the safety of employees addressed, it is easier to focus on addressing the other areas of your disaster recovery plan. Ensuring they can exit the building if necessary is fundamental. Equipment and data will not be of any use if employees are not around after the disaster. Building an emergency information list with phone numbers for each employee along with persons to contact in the event of an emergency will add peace of mind. Reaching individuals on the emergency notification list will ensure that the necessary people are provided with good information rather than being kept in the dark.

Disseminating Disaster Information: A Unique Twist on a Web Site

Dissemination of information to employees who are off-site during an emergency can be problematic, especially if something happens to on-site records. The nonprofit's existing infrastructure, or in this case the lack thereof, can be useful. In the spring 2003 survey found in Appendix A, 97% of all nonprofit respondents indicated they had a web site and 88% of those organizations have the web site hosted by another organization, which means it is housed off-site. Having the site hosted externally can serve as an advantage for nonprofits. An externally hosted web site could serve as the vehicle to pass vital information to employees in the event of a disaster at their place of operation without having to sink funds into developing a strategy or creating a mechanism. An emergency announcement can be tucked away on a web site so employees can retrieve it when necessary. During the short-term recovery phase of a disaster recovery plan, the web site can be updated with important information and employees can be directed to it. A nonprofit has two major choices for implementation:

1. *Post a hidden emergency page.* The nonprofit can store a single web page on the site with no links pointing to the page. (The page could be left up and running at all times or it could be pre-made and uploaded to the web site during the first stages of short-term recovery.) A user could access the information by entering the entire path of the URL into

a web browser. For example, an employee may direct his or her browser to: http://www.charityname.org/drp/1/ emergency_contacts_and_info.htm to gain information regarding a nonprofit's response to a snow emergency. Since the normal pages of the web site would not have any navigation buttons or links to the disaster recovery page, the general public would not even know of its existence. The complexity of the URL provides a certain level of security while making information available to employees.

2. *Secure information with scripting or use an extranet.* Those organizations which would desire a more secure manner of posting information would be able to secure the information with a form of scripting, such as Active Server Pages, Perl, or by using an extranet. The disaster recovery team should consult the IT department and/or the vendor which is hosting the web site to determine which solution would be ideal for the nonprofit.

Being able to quickly and efficiently share information between employees will lessen confusion and aid the nonprofit in moving through the immediate response on to short- and long-term recovery procedures.

Don't Just Get Insurance, Talk To the Insurance Company

A member of the disaster recovery team should talk with the nonprofit's insurance company *before* a crisis and discuss some key issues.

Understand what is specifically covered and not covered in the insurance policy. Finding out what is covered when filing a claim is too late (although it happens). Make adjustments to the policy so all employees (and volunteers, if appropriate), emergency operational expenses, essential equipment, and the facility, itself, are covered. If your organization conducts off-site volunteer events, they may need to be covered as well. Establishing the proper level of coverage is extremely important, however it is only the first step in obtaining insurance security.

The nonprofit will need to know what is necessary in order to process a claim before a disaster occurs. Identify what is necessary for proof of ownership and proof of loss. Every insurance company has their own requirements. Many insurance companies will require that an up to date inventory be submitted and remain on file. Others may accept copies of original receipts and a list of serial numbers at the time of the claim. In the case of computers, some insurance companies prefer an itemized list with an original purchase price and a photograph of the equipment. The key point here is to know rather than assume what *your* insurance company requires. It would be a tragedy to have insurance and have a claim denied. For some nonprofits, that would be enough to close their doors forever.

Questions for Review and Implementation

1. What characteristics are essential of a disaster recovery team leader and who would meet those characteristics in your organization? Would it be necessary to hire a consultant?
2. What should be covered in a disaster recovery plan?
3. What are a nonprofit's most valuable assets?
4. What is the difference between systems that are vital, important, and useful?
5. Why is it necessary to include members from different parts of the organization on the disaster recovery team?
6. What information should be included in a personnel contact sheet?
7. How can Internet technology play a role in information dissemination?
8. What type of information is required to show proof-of-ownership and proof-of-loss to your insurance company?

Chapter 3
Protecting Information and Functions

The majority of this chapter addresses identifying both the vital pieces of information belonging to the nonprofit and the functions of the nonprofit, itself. Many disaster recovery plans which are technologically based or are sole projects of an IT department may neglect covering non-electronic forms of data. Of course it is important to be concerned with computer data and the functions performed by a PC or server, but a nonprofit has many other pieces of information that are vital and in some instances required by law in order for the nonprofit to be able to function. Care needs to be taken about safeguarding all of the nonprofit's information.

Document Backups: Hard or Electronic Copies?

Before diving into the subject of what data and procedures are to be secured, a special note should be given to the options for securing the information, i.e., the mechanism and the medium to be used. Nonprofits have two major choices in backing up information: hard or electronic/digital copies. The method employed is ultimately a matter of convenience to the organization.

Much of the information described in this chapter exists in paper form. The source documents, which usually originate from a computer, will not contain two important items: signatures and dates. Tax statements and contracts need to be signed and dated in order to be valid. Saving copies of electronic documents in Microsoft® Word® or WordPerfect® may be helpful, but those electronic files will not contain the binding power of the signed documents. It will be necessary to work with the final, signed, and dated documents. As a result, the nonprofit will need to handle paper documents, possibly in large volume. Copies of the documents described in the next several sections will need to be made. The nonprofit will need to copy documents in their entirety, which may include copying double-sided pages. Do not accidentally neglect key pages of information. In this matter, the disaster recovery team will need to decide how information and records will be stored, i.e., hard copies generated by a photocopier or digital copies which will be generated from a scanner.

There are benefits to creating hard copies of documents. Most offices have photocopiers, which generate copies at fast rates, and the hard copies can be read without the use of a computer. The primary disadvantages of these hard copies are the amount of space the documents may consume and the cost of copying many pages. Nonprofits may not have an off-site facility available to store boxes of documents.

Digital document scanning is an alternative which offers a different set of advantages. Scanned documents can easily be stored and organized on local storage devices such as hard drives or servers, or moved to compact discs (CD) and then copies can be printed as needed. CDs do not take up large amounts of space and multiple copies of the CDs can be made and distributed to disaster recovery team members. The disadvantages of digital documents are that it requires special equipment to create the files, the process is not as fast as a photocopier, and a computer will be needed to access the information. Nonprofits might think that the cost of obtaining a scanner with a document feeder and a re-writable CD-ROM drive is cost prohibitive. But consider this: the cost of this equipment is currently less than $800. Photocopying and paper expenses on leased equipment might be comparable if a large number of documents need to be saved.

If the nonprofit chooses to save digital copies of its information, it will need to consider the type of medium on to which the information will be stored and in what format the files will be saved. Consider storing the information on a CD or DVD rather than on to a tape or diskette. CDs, which hold approximately 650MB, which is the equivalent of over 8,000 pages stored in Adobe®'s Portable Document Format (PDF), can be read by nearly all personal computers. DVDs offer even greater storage capacity. Floppy disks on the other hand, which only last for approximately five years, hold approximately 18 pages stored as a PDF. Saving the documents to a backup tape might require the use of special equipment to read the tape and not make the information accessible when time is of the essence. Tapes and diskettes are magnetic media which will do not have as long a shelf life as a CDs.

With a scanned document there are a number of file formats into which the data can be stored. The nonprofit should scan its documents with good print quality (300 dpi or better) and choose to store its digital documents in a widely used format such as PDF, rather than as an art file or word processing file. PDFs have been around for years and are widely used, the files can be read by both PCs and Macintosh computers, and the Adobe® Acrobat® reader is a free download available on the Internet (http://www.adobe.com). The full version of Acrobat®, which is used to both read and create PDFs is available for approximately $200.

The library of saved documents will be important in the disaster recovery plans of a nonprofit. Many of the documents are often overlooked by nonprofits when preparing a plan. No matter which system is used, the end result should be the same: the documents should be stored in a secure location, easily accessible, and easily updatable. Some details on these matters appears in Chapter 5. In deciding which methods to use to back up data, the nonprofit should consider the types of information to be stored and the quantities of material, which will be outlined next.

Protecting the Organization's Records

As a matter of normal operating and legal practice, nonprofits and their commercial counterparts are required to keep track of key pieces of information on a regular basis. The record retention policy for nonprofits, however, is different than the policies used in the commercial sector. For example, a federal mandate from the IRS that went into effect on June 8, 1999 requires nonprofits to have certain documents available for public inspection. These include the nonprofit's application for exemption, IRS Form 1023, supporting documents, and the last three years' worth of annual information returns, which include IRS Forms 990, 990-EZ, 990-BL, and 1065. It also includes, generally, all schedules and attachments filed with the IRS. These documents, which have been identified by the IRS for public disclosure, appear in 26 CFR (Code of Federal Regulations) Part 301 and 602. Preserving this information in a disaster is not a matter of convenience, but rather one of necessity. If a nonprofit organization models its disaster recovery plan blindly on the plan of a commercial organization, several pieces of information will be missed, like the ones mentioned. A nonprofit should create a checklist of essential documents to be backed up. The items on a nonprofit's checklist should include the legal documents of the organization and may contain additional information which pertain to the specific organization. A sample list appears in Table 3.1.

Table 3.1 – Nonprofit Information Checklist

- The corporate record book, which includes:
  - Incorporation documents
  - By-laws
  - Tax-exemption documents including the application for tax exemption (IRS Form 1023), the IRS determination letter, and related documents
  - Board meeting documents including agendas, minutes, and related documents
  - Year end treasurer's financial report or statement
- Financial documents, which include:
  - Seven years' worth of annual information returns (IRS Form 990, 990-EZ, 990-BL, or 1065)
  - Three years' worth of annual treasurer's reports
  - Seven years' worth of bank statements, canceled checks, check registers, investment statements and related documents
- State charitable registration documents

- Personnel records
- Insurance forms with policy numbers
- *Signed* contracts with vendors
- Depending on the nonprofit organization, it may be necessary to retain scholarship records.

Applicable Regulations

Disaster recovery planning is a practice which is indirectly affected by regulations. Several federal and IRS regulations require commercial entities to maintain certain types of data records. While none of the following laws pertain specifically to nonprofit organizations, the laws were adopted to cover all industries. It might be worthwhile to have a legal advisor review the documents to make sure the nonprofit organization does not have any liabilities. For example, if a nonprofit receives donations online or receives donations via a monthly giving program using Electronic Funds Transfer (EFT), the nonprofit may want to review what material needs to be stored as identified by the Consumer Credit Protection Act (CCPA) of 1992. The CCPA specifically governs e-commerce transactions, which is relatively new to many nonprofit organizations. Additional laws appear in Table 3.2.

Table 3.2 – Laws Affecting Records Retention

Law	Issue
Consumer Credit Protection Act of 1992	Outlines due diligence for availability of data in Electronic Fund Transfers (EFT) including Point of Sale.
Foreign Corrupt Practices Act of 1977	While specifically addressing the international transfer of money and bribery, it also establishes management accountability through record keeping.
IRS Procedure 86-19	Establishes legal backup and recovery requirements for computer records containing tax data.

Protecting the Organization's Activities

Audits should be conducted to identify every system and process in the day-to-day operation of the nonprofit. Once each activity has been identified, a Standard Operating Procedure (SOP) should be written. An SOP should contain five pieces of information:

1. How to perform a particular activity
2. Who the responsible party is that performs the given action
3. What equipment and material is necessary to perform the procedure. Access to a custom database, the nonprofit's stationery/letterhead, bank deposit slips, etc., that are necessary to perform work.
4. The level of importance of the activity to the organization – this is assigned by the disaster recovery team
5. The date the SOP was created and by whom

All too often nonprofits rely on the memories of employees rather than forming an institutional memory. "How is that done again?"..."Oh, I don't know – ask Jane. She's been here forever." It is important to document procedures. Writing SOPs, especially for large nonprofits, is an overwhelming task. It is impossible for all of them to be prepared by one individual as no one person has the knowledge of every activity in the organization. SOPs should be prepared by different people throughout the organization. That is part of the reason for having a disaster recovery team. SOPs should give enough guidance so anyone in the organization would have the general framework to begin work in that role. An example of an SOP appears in Figure 3.1. This SOP describes the process of receiving donations, which is important to many nonprofits. There are a number of interesting points to note in this example.

1. The steps in the process are outlined, but not to the point of giving specific instructions. This will make the document valuable and will extend the life span of the SOP. Instructions on how to operate the donor database are not given here and nor should they be. If the nonprofit changes systems or databases, this SOP will remain functional. If there was a high level of detail on how to operate the computer, the SOP would quickly become obsolete.

2. The instructions provide enough detail to be clear. For example, the high dollar donation level is specifically stated as $100.

3. Note how the responsible party is identified by the position and not by the person's name. This again adds to the life span of the SOP. It will not need to be changed if an employee leaves the organization or gets promoted to a new position.

4. The required systems/materials are specifically identified. This will help the disaster recovery team target specific systems to bring up and running first. It is possible that several SOPs will list the same required system making a particular item targeted for immediate or short-term recovery rather than long-term recovery.

5. This SOP has creation and revision dates as well as the names of the creator and the person who gave the SOP approval.

SOPs will vary in degrees of complexity depending on what is involved. A map of the network layout may be more involved than the procedure of communicating to volunteers of an annual event. Both are vital to the nonprofit, but each is intrinsically different.

Creating SOPs will take time and often get pushed aside for more demanding work. It is the responsibility of the disaster recovery team leader to coordinate efforts with various employees and establish reasonable deadlines. All SOPs will not be developed at the same time, but care should be given to make sure they do not fall through the cracks. When all of the SOPs have been submitted, the disaster recovery team should identify the rank of each SOP and then prepare a list of all equipment/materials in order of importance of the system. Not all activities can receive the same vital status. Each department will feel that their particular systems are the most important. By looking at all of the SOPs from an overall perspective, the systems can be weighed against one another.

With all of the SOPs created, an outsider or auditor should be able to identify all of the activities of an organization and the equipment necessary to carry out those functions. A good checks-

Figure 3.1 – Sample SOP

Disaster Recovery Plan
Standard Operating Procedure

Processing a Donation

Required systems/materials:
            Access to the donor database on the network
            Access to a network workstation
            Letterhead
            Welcome package
            Bank deposit slip

Responsible party: Assistant to the Director of Development

Procedure: 1.   Record the name of the donor, address, e-mail address,
                    date, and donation amount in the donor database.
              2.   Notify the director if the gift is a high-dollar donation,
                    i.e., a gift greater than $100.
              3.   Prepare an acknowledgement letter on the nonprofit's
                    stationery.
              4.   If the donor is new to the organization, include a
                    welcome package with the acknowledgement.
              5.   Prepare a bank deposit slip with the week's donations
                    every Thursday afternoon.
              6.   Log and store the bank receipt.

Created by: _Madeline DeFelice_ Date created: ___May 6, 2001___

Approved by: ___Jane Fulcher___   Last revision: ___Dec. 8, 2003___

System importance:___Vital___

and-balances system is to work backwards. Identify all of the equipment in the facility and make sure it has a corresponding task. Some equipment such as ventilation systems or plumbing will have no associated tasks, but will be important to the organization. Do not forget to include them in the final list of equipment.

Protecting Sources of Income

Commercial organizations will approach forming a disaster recovery plan differently than their nonprofit counterparts. For-profits will need to ensure the continuous delivery of products and services to maintain its customer base. Downtime will result not only in repair costs, but lost revenue as well. Nonprofit income is generated by different mechanisms. While there are products and services provided, they do not generate revenue. Nonprofits generate revenue from donations or gifts made to the organization. Individual contributions account for 76% of all contributions to nonprofits (AAFRC Trust for Philanthropy, 2002). Other sources of income include corporate gifts and grants from government agencies or foundations. Nonprofits will need to protect their fundraising efforts during disaster recovery planning. In many cases, this will include protecting information and, if applicable, gifts-in-kind. Items to target in the plan include:

- Lists of benefactors/donors will need to be backed up. In many instances this will require the backup of a database. Specific detail is given to electronic data in the next section of this chapter.
- Grant applications take considerable time and expertise to prepare. Copies of applications and their supporting documents should be made.
- Gifts-in-kind should be stored at a safe location with proper security against theft, fire, and natural disaster. An inventory of items should be complete and the items should be properly insured.
- If the nonprofit conducts fundraising by means of written or printed material (such as direct mail), a set of logos, letterhead, and artwork should be backed up. Nonprofits often pay considerable time and money developing and testing a publicly recognized image. These branding efforts should be

Case History:
The Value of a Backup

A small company located Pennsylvania experienced a hard drive crash in 1993. The company was not in the practice of backing up the individual PCs in the office. The drive was sent to a specialty shop where it was determined after approximately one week that virtually nothing was recoverable. All of the company's financial records were lost. One month was spent recreating the lost spreadsheets.

safeguarded. A nonprofit would not want to be forced to change its image and sense of public trust based on an accident.

Nonprofits are constantly searching for new sources of revenue and ways to improve their existing processes. Immediately following a disaster, whether large or small, the nonprofit may wish to perform an emergency appeal seeking help. This effort might be nearly impossible if one or more of the above items is lost.

Backing Up Electronic Data

It is becoming increasingly vital for nonprofits to back up computer data. Doing work by computer is not just a matter of convenience any more – it is essential. An example is with state registrations. The state of Colorado now requires charities, which solicit funds to its residents, to register online. Computers are an integral part of nonprofit business and as a result computer data needs to be backed up.

One of the most promising statistics in the spring 2003 survey is the one addressing computer backups. 97% of respondents backup some portion of their computer files. Even with this high number, several items need to be addressed, such as data, applications, operating systems, and frequency. There are a wide variety of backup techniques available to nonprofits to ensure the safety of their computer software and data. While the concept of backing up files is not difficult to understand – making an exact copy of a file to a separate location – in practice it is sometimes a little more advanced and as a result there are some special considerations need to be mentioned.

Data

When a nonprofit backs up its computer data, it should be sure to get all of it. This statement may seem simple enough and even a bit absurd. But the hidden aspects of it may prove otherwise. Computer users have a tendency to store files in all sorts of places. Data might be stored on a network server as requested by an IT department. And at the same time, much to an IT manager's dismay, some of it could also be in several locations on a local hard drive, such as the desktop or in "My Documents" of a Windows®-based computer. Data can even find its way to the personal archives on someone's bookshelf in the form of floppy disks or CDs. It is as if the data grows feet and starts walking around. Users will often save files in a way that is most convenient for them; not for the IT department. A slow network or complicated file tree might not be the preferred place to store information from the users' points of view. This will be problematic when it comes time to back up files. The disaster recovery team will need to ensure that all of the nonprofit's data is backed up on a regular basis. (Remember those audits from the last chapter? It is time to do some more to find all of the data.) This may mean backing up data from servers and from workstations. If a nonprofit can guarantee that no data is stored on local workstations, then there is no need to include them in the routine backup. A network-based system might make it possible for backup software to reach all of the PCs. In the event that an office is equipped with stand-alone PCs or the backup software cannot access the individual machines other than the server(s) it is installed on, one of two things (or even both) needs to be done.

1. Back up the data from each computer. This may require each user to be responsible for his or her own backup, it may require several licensed copies of backup software, or it may require one person each week to make the rounds to different workstations. It does not matter which method is used so long as the data is secured. The best method is the one which is most convenient to the users and to the person responsible for performing the backup. This solution is not ideal for a large office.
2. Require the users to store their data on a common device that can be backed up and then back up the data from that device. This solution works well for a network-based

system where the backup software works on a few PCs or a few servers, but cannot reach every PC. If the backup software can not get to the data, bring the data to the software. There are a number of solutions available to bring users into compliance. The implemented policy can be an employee policy or a technical solution. In the event that the employees do not always remember to follow through with the instructions, computers can be set up in such a way to help them along. For example, the default file storage locations for programs such as Microsoft® Word® and Excel® can be modified. These applications normally point to the "My Documents" folder of the local hard drive. They can be changed under the "Options" menu to point to a shared volume on the network. Workstations can be equipped with policies to force users to store files on a common computer. Some users may feel confined, but the strategy is being done for the good of the organization.

Special consideration needs to be given to those data files that are in continual use. Any file which is in use by a program will be locked and it will not normally be possible for a backup system to gain access to back it up. Many nonprofits would think this category does not really apply to them, because after all, most workers are not in the facility during the middle of the night when the automated backup is being performed. This, however, is not always the case. Many nonprofits make use of these types of files. Three examples of files, which are typically open, are databases, e-mail systems, and operating system software. Databases such as Microsoft's® SQL® Server and those attached to a web site, which receive donations or newsletter updates, are continuously open. E-mail servers, which are in a constant ready state, are always open. If a server is running 24/7, there are files that are open and in use. If these data files are in constant use, many backup programs will be unable to successfully create a backup. Even more bothersome is the trait of some backup programs to not notify the user of such an occurrence. In order to backup files in use, backup software packages need to be specifically designed to handle open files, for example Backup Exec® by Veritas® has designed a component for this situation called Open File Option®. Disaster recovery teams will need to ensure that open files are secured, especially since the information stored in those types of databases and e-mail systems is the livelihood of the organization.

Applications

Nonprofits should, by all means, back up their data. In the event that a server crashes or there is a system failure, a secure copy of data can be the difference between continued success or the nightmare of failure. As a nonprofit begins to back up its data, it should ensure that the data will be accessible if it is restored to a different or new system. In order for the data to be valuable, the program that is used to access the file must also be available. Nonprofits, therefore, need to make backups of their applications as well.

If a nonprofit uses standard commercial software, copies of the original installation CD, the product key, serial number, and EULA (End User License Agreement) should be made. If on the other hand the nonprofit uses custom software or software that is no longer sold or supported, a copy of the application from the server

Case History:
Backing More Than Just Data:

Recently there was a small nonprofit in the Washington, DC area that experienced a small disaster. One PC in the office crashed and the hard drive needed to be replaced. On that PC were some old data files. The data files were meticulously backed-up every night like clock-work. The day after the computer crashed, the floppy diskette with the data magically appeared and all of the data was found to be secure. But before the victory celebration could ensue, it was discovered that the application software used to access the files, which was no longer being sold or supported by the manu-facturer, was nowhere to be found. The backup proved to be utterly useless. As a result, several weeks' worth of work had to be spent reconstructing the necessary files. Applications are just as essential as data at times.

or PC will need to be made. Care should be made to backup the entire application and system settings so the program can be restored to a new computer. If the nonprofit uses legacy or custom software that requires an older OS, such as MS-DOS, which is no longer supported, care should be made to back it up.

Operating Systems

While data is at the heart of many systems, the operating system (OS) which is used to run the computers is equally as important. It is not possible to access the data without it. Additionally, current OSs are expensive. Most OSs are sold with PCs and servers and are already installed. In the event that the nonprofit needs to only replace storage devices on these machines, it will be possible to re-install the OS. Nonprofits may choose during the recovery process following a disaster to either install an OS from their original source or restore the OS from the backup. In the event of a re-install, care should be given to make a backup of the OS discs, product keys, serial numbers, and EULAs (to prove ownership). At a time when a speedy recovery is preferred, restoring from backup may be the way to go.

Backing up an OS (and some applications) will require an extra step beyond what is normally done for data files. The registry, which is a special component of the Microsoft® Windows® and Novell® Netware® OSs will need to be backed up as well. The registry contains essential information about the setup and configuration of the OS and applications. If a nonprofit were to restore an OS and applications from its backup without restoring the registry, the programs would not be able to run correctly. The procedure to backup and restore a registry, which is not always part of a normal backup procedure by default, is fully explained at Microsoft®'s TechNet® website (http://www.microsoft.com/technet) and at Novell®'s support site (http://www.support.novell.com). In some instances, it is possible to reinstall an OS and applications from their original CDs and then restore the data for the applications from backup.

How to Back Up and How Often?

Nonprofits have several choices available to them when it comes to determining the backup frequency of their electronic systems. The driving principle behind determining how frequently to back up files is to make the backups often enough so that none or only a minimal amount of data would be lost if a restore were to be conducted. Applications and OSs may need to be backed up only when there are configuration changes. Data on the other hand may need to be backed up on a daily or more frequent basis. Daily backups of data would mean in a worst case scenario, only one day's worth of data would be missing in the event of a disaster. The longer a nonprofit goes between backups, the more time will need to be spent during the recovery phase on rebuilding data.

Full backups appear to be the most common. Nonprofits have the option to use incremental or differential. These back up only those files that have changed since the last backup. Faster backup process is with incremental and differential, but they are the slowest types of backups to restore. All of the tapes since the last full backup will be required. More is explained in *Backup Methods.*

Storage Mediums

After identifying what to back up, a nonprofit will need to decide on to what medium the data should be stored. Several options are available, each with its own unique set of benefits and characteristics. Which medium a nonprofit uses depends on issues such as ease of use, permanency, and price. Files which are to be stored permanently, such as articles of incorporation, tax exempt applications, and by-laws should be stored on a long lasting medium such as a CD. The main drawback to using CDs is that once they have been created, the data which is on them is permanent. Re-writable CDs have a compatibility issue of working only in re-writable CD-ROM drives. Magnetic mediums, such as cartridges, tapes, and diskettes, which offer the ability to be easily updated and re-written, are not permanent. Magnetic fields and excessive use can degrade the quality and reliability of medium, which will eventually render it inoperable. The magnetic field on a tape or diskette will eventually decay. These storage devices do not last forever. The benefit, however, is their ability to be re-used.

The price of the different mediums varies greatly. If a nonprofit is looking to implement a backup device, the cost of media will may play a factor. Not only does the initial cost of the backup device vary, but so does the cost of the medium, itself. CDs, while they can only be used once, are the cheapest storage medium available. Table 3.3 lists various mediums, their native storage capacity, i.e., without compressed data, and their price as they appeared in March 2003.

Another option available to nonprofits is electronic vaulting. In this process of backing up data, the information to be secured is transmitted to an electronic tape library at an off-site location such as Iron Mountain® and LiveVault®. The data is housed at a safe location at their facility, and if needed, the data can be delivered to the nonprofit. This makes the data off-site, off-line, and out-of-reach. This backup method may be cost prohibitive for many nonprofits and may not be the ideal method for securing the data if the nonprofit needs to retrieve the files from backup after minor incidents. Here is an example shared by an anonymous nonprofit in Maryland during late 2002. About once a month, under a dozen files needed to be retrieved from backup tape after a recurring, small disaster: a user kept deleting the files unintentionally. Having to pay to have the data retrieved from an electronic vault would have been cost prohibitive. In this story, the nonprofit retrieved the files from the off-site backup tape. The so called disaster has since been corrected through a novel technique: end-user education. Electronic vaulting is a valuable resource that has its place. It may prove very appropriate for a larger disaster.

Table 3.3 – Cost of Storage Medium

Medium	Storage Capacity	List Price	Cost/MB
Zip Disk	100 or 250 MB	$10	$0.04
CD-R	650 MB	$0.40	$0.0006
Cartridge	10 GB (not compressed)	$100	$0.01
Tape	20 GB (not compressed)	$50	$0.0025

Backup Method

There are three primary backup methods available: full, differential, and incremental. Of those nonprofits which backed up their data according to the spring 2003 survey, 74% backup their files by means of a full backup. Full backups take the longest amount of time to complete and occupy the largest amount of space as it copies all of the selected files to another medium, such as a tape. Every time the backup is performed all of the selected files are recopied, those files that have changed since the previous backup and even those files which have not changed since the previous backup. This backup procedure does spend a significant amount of time re-backing up the same material. While this backup method takes the most time to complete of the three, it is the most convenient for retrieving files. Only one set of tapes is necessary to restore the files and the most recent tape will contain the most up to date information.

Differential and incremental backups do not copy all selected files every time the procedure is performed. In a differential backup any file which has been altered since *the last full backup* is copied to the backup medium. In order to perform a restore, the last full backup is restored to the computer and then the last differential backup is also restored. The two sets are required to give the complete picture of the system prior to the disaster.

In an incremental backup any file which has changed since the previous backup is copied to the backup medium. Normally a full backup is performed and then a series of incremental backups are performed over the next several days. Each incremental backup copies only the files that have changed since the previous day. In the event of a restore, the full backup must be restored and then every incremental backup must be restored in the order in which they were made. All sets are necessary to restore the full system.

The chief advantages to using either of the differential or incremental methods is that the backup process, itself, takes less time to complete after the initial full backup. These methods also require less storage media as they only backup changed files. The major drawback to these methods is the number of tapes required to complete the full file restoration. In both of these methods multiple tape sets are required to restore the full system. Aside from taking more time to perform the restoration procedure, there is another concern. If something should happen to the full backup or one of the differential or incremental backup sets, depending on which method is used, the restore process will not work. A nonprofit may choose to weigh its choices. Table 3.4 outlines the three backup methods and their pros and cons.

Nonprofits have a considerable amount of information to be backed up for their disaster recovery plans. This information exists in different forms and is most likely scattered throughout the organization. The purpose of backing up this information is to not only meet the necessary regulations, but also to provide a secure institutional memory. Electronic data is only one aspect of the data to be secured, but is increasingly vital because of the way nonprofits conduct their business. Backups need to be made of data, applications, and operating systems if the nonprofit hopes to restore full system to a full operational status after a disaster. There are a

Table 3.4 – Backup Methods

Method	Full	Differential	Incremental
Backup Action	Copies all files	Copies only those files which have changed since the last full backup	Copies only those files which have changed since the last incremental back-up
Backup Time	Longest backup procedure	Relatively short backup procedure	Shortest backup procedure
Storage Space	Occupies the most storage media	Occupies less space than full backup	Occupies the least amount of storage media
Restore Require-ments	Requires only the most recent backup to perform a full restoration	Requires the most recent full backup and the most recent differential back-up to perform a full restoration	Requires the most recent full backup and all of the incremental backups made since the last full backup for a full restoration
Restore Time	Takes the least amount of time to perform a full restore	Takes more time to complete a full restoration when compared to a full backup	Takes the most time to complete a full restoration of all three methods

number of techniques and approaches available to nonprofit organizations. A nonprofit will need to pick the approach and method which is right for its budget and operational needs. Protecting the information and functions are vital to the disaster recovery plan. The more complete the information, the better the chances that systems can be restored in a short amount of time.

Questions for Review and Implementation

1. What methods are available for a nonprofit to backup its vital documents?
2. What records must be maintained by a nonprofit for public inspecttion?
3. What information should be listed on a nonprofit's information checklist?
4. Are there any regulations or laws that apply to disaster recovery?
5. What is institutional memory?
6. What is the purpose of a Standard Operating Procedure?
7. What can a nonprofit do to protect its sources of income?
8. What difficulties hinder the backing up of electronic data?
9. What special considerations need to be identified in backing up applications and operating systems?
10. How frequently should a nonprofit back up its data?
11. What mediums are currently available for performing backups?
12. What are the three types of backups typically available to nonprofits and what are the pros and cons associated with each?

Chapter 4
Risks: Inside and Out

When people first start working on the risk analyses portion of their disaster recovery plans, many individuals bring to mind images of a bunch of nay-sayers and pessimists sitting in a room thinking of all the bad things that can happen. Unfortunately this is a very glum outlook of the process for both the disaster recovery team and the nonprofit's employees. It may also be a reason why disaster recovery planning hasn't been implemented by more organizations. In the 2003 survey, only 50% of those organizations who had a disaster recovery plan in place conducted risk analyses. These tools are very important elements of disaster recovery plans. They prevent team members from being disillusioned into false security or from becoming too myopic. It is very difficult to implement a disaster recovery plan without the information obtained in this process. These analyses, rather than bringing down the morale of the team and employees, have the opportunity to strengthen the nonprofit's position by allowing for preventative measures to be developed, for the formation of contingency plans, and for diversification.

As the time comes to analyze the potential threats that face a nonprofit, the task may appear overwhelming because of all of the various possibilities. The number of disasters that can strike a charity is virtually endless. But before creating a monstrous list, it is helpful to understand the purpose of risk analyses, which is two-fold. They are to identify the likely or probable threats that:

1.   Would prohibit, prevent, or hinder a nonprofit from providing its services, i.e., the fulfillment of the nonprofit's mission statement, and
2.   Would adversely effect the generation of revenue, which in turn would make it impossible for the nonprofit to provide programs or services.

Some people view the second item mentioned above as an element of a business contingency plan, but it will be presented here because of its importance and unique characteristics pertaining to the nonprofit sector.

What could possibly go wrong? That's the general theme behind conducting risk analyses and their assessments. Securing data, documents, and standard operating procedures, which were the themes covered thus far, are only the first steps in preparing a disaster recovery plan. With the threats to the operations of a nonprofit identified, the disaster recovery team is in a fortunate position to:

1.   Remove existing threats,
2.   Minimize weaknesses, and
3.   Be prepared to handle disastrous situations.

The information harvested from risk analyses may require a nonprofit to revise some of the previously developed plans, SOPs, and documentation. This is a good thing. This is a sign that the disaster recovery team is correcting plans as assumptions are revised.

Starting Points

A disaster recovery team could choose from a number of different starting points in the identification of risks, but there is some information to guide them in their way so they can make the most of their time and efforts. Some industry statistics have been identified in key areas which can serve as focal points. Rather than focus on a million different scenarios, a nonprofit should begin by identifying those threats − both internal and external − which are more likely to occur than others. A perfect disaster recovery plan will be all encompassing and be ready to address any disaster, but nonprofits rarely have the time and money to develop a perfect plan. The viable alternative is to build a very strong plan with the resources allotted that will address likely scenarios of system-wide failure. By examining those threats which are more likely to occur, a nonprofit can focus its energy on specific systems. Take forest fires as an example. Forest fires are devastating events that wipe out acres of property and destroy buildings in the near vicinity. A nonprofit located in New York City will not need to address the likelihood of being adversely affected by a forest fire (unless it relates to their mission). A nonprofit in the suburbs will probably not be as concerned about city-related incidents such as the interruption of public transportation. The nonprofit's team should keep a healthy perspective as it moves through the various procedures outlined below.

Procedures

The actual risk analysis procedure is not very complicated, but in order for it to be effective, it needs to be thorough, organized, and insightful. Keeping the previous statements about the purpose of risk analyses in mind will also be helpful. The first step in the process is to identify all of the threats that exist for the nonprofit, both internal and external. A sample list appears in Table 4.1. The disaster recovery team should feel free to be creative and list all possibilities, no matter how crazy they might first seem. This list will be the basis for future steps so it is important to make it as extensive as possible. Some times it is helpful to think in reverse, i.e., to look at the various systems and procedures and determine how they can be interrupted.

After a full and exhaustive list has been prepared by the disaster recovery team, several additional elements will need to be added to the list. The second piece of data to be identified is the probability of each disaster occurring. Some of this information will be subject to speculation because no one can predict if and when a disaster will occur. At this point, employees and members of the team may begin to question the worthiness of developing a disaster recovery plan. Developing a plan will require significant resources

Table 4.1 – Potential Risks

Fire	Lightning strike
Flood	Nuclear incident
Tornado	Theft of equipment
Hurricane	Theft of information
Earthquake	Computer virus/hack
Power outage	Employee turnover
Tsunami	Financial scandal
Terrorist attack	Vandalism
Volcano	Loss of utility services
Snow/ice storm	Loss of Phone/Internet connection

be expended and the probability of a disastrous situation occurring may seem remote. It is absolutely important to remember that disaster recovery plans are not built based on the odds of an occurrence happening, but rather they are built on the significance of the impact of such events. Nonprofits cannot afford to play the odds. What drives the formation of plans is the consequence of not having a strong enough plan in place when a disaster does occur (Pelant, 2003).

In order to guide the nonprofit in its thinking it will be helpful to conduct additional research. Many state emergency management agencies can provide regional statistics on weather related events such as the frequency of tornados, hurricanes, lightning strikes, etc. Local police departments can provide statistics on theft and vandalism. If the nonprofit is located in a place that is susceptible to certain types of events, those items should receive a higher probability rating. Identifying the probability of a disaster will help focus the actions of a disaster recovery team.

Probability, however, is not the only significant factor in risk analysis. The next several pieces of information are equally important. The third piece of information to be added will be

> Case History:
> The Value of Security
>
> A small nonprofit in Washington, DC, relocated its offices across town. In May of 2002, on the first night when all of the computer equipment was moved on-site, there was an incident. The office space adjacent to the nonprofit was broken into. The thieves then broke through the wall adjoining the two offices. The nonprofit lost all of their computer equipment – PCs, server, and printers. All of the electronic data was lost as the nonprofit did not have a backup of their material.

overlayed on top of the first. The disaster recovery team should identify the severity of the impact of each disaster listed as it applies to both the nonprofit as a whole and on particular systems. Certain types of disasters may be localized to particular tools/systems used by the nonprofit, such as utilities and computer networks while others may affect the entire building. The result of combining the information from steps one through three should result in something similar to the sample presented in Figure 4.1.

With these three pieces of information combined, the disaster recovery team has a useful tool that can identify those disasters which should receive the most attention and be immediately addressed by the recovery plan. If the team were to plot a graph of each incident by its probability of occurrence by the vital systems affected, a graph will be created which identifies the

Figure 4.1 – Risk Analysis Chart from Steps One through Three

Risk Analysis			
Disaster	Probability of occurring	Severity of disaster	Impacted Systems
Fire	_____	_____	_____
Flood	_____	_____	_____
Tornado	_____	_____	_____
Hurricane	_____	_____	_____
Earthquake	_____	_____	_____
Power outage	_____	_____	_____
Tsunami	_____	_____	_____
Volcano	_____	_____	_____
Snow/ice storm	_____	_____	_____
Nuclear disaster	_____	_____	_____
Theft of info	_____	_____	_____
Theft of equip	_____	_____	_____
Computer virus/hack	_____	_____	_____
Vandalism	_____	_____	_____
Loss of phone/Internet	_____	_____	_____
Vandalism	_____	_____	_____
Employee turnover	_____	_____	_____

Figure 4.2 – Risk Analysis Graph

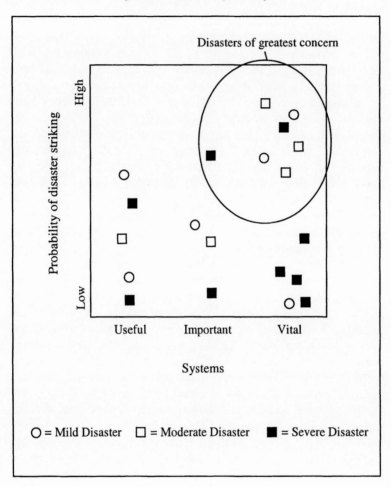

areas of most concern. Figure 4.2 shows a sample graph of events. The items on the right side of the graph indicate areas of concern and the items in the upper right portion of the graph are of top concern as they are not only likely to occur, but have the ability to affect vital systems. The lower right portion of the graph will have the highest number of severe disasters, but these events – such as tornados, earthquakes, and hurricanes – usually have lower probabilities of occurring. (This may not necessarily be true for the location of your charity.)

After identifying the risks to which a nonprofit is exposed, the final piece of information for analysis can be added. This piece will be the most action-oriented of all of the procedures and will lead the disaster recovery team into the implementation of the disaster recovery plan. Starting with the disasters of most concern, the disaster recovery team should attempt to identify if any of the disasters can be avoided or minimized by implementing preventative measures. The information generated in this portion of the process will be initially cursory of nature, but its significance will dictate that two steps logically ensue: 1.) That detailed information will be formed about the possible preventive measures, and 2.) The information becomes part of the action plans for implementation. Not all disasters can be avoided, such as tornados or floods, but the effects of disasters and the development of a recovery plan can be created.

Risk analysis tends to start with broad sweeping strokes and then moves to finite details. As additional logic and information is introduced into the analysis, more logical outcomes can be reached which will identify appropriate courses of action. An example of a broad sweeping statement is to say that a computer network could go down. That statement can then be further refined to say that the accounting department's software can become corrupt, thereby rendering the users without a system to conduct billing. There are a number of other refinements that can also be made about the network and the accounting software, itself. This type of refinement is achieved through the step-wise process just described. It can be applied to the many systems – computer driven and not – which are used by the nonprofit. Since computer systems are so widely used and because more and more vital activities of nonprofits are taking place on them, additional information on computer systems will be explored.

Computer Systems

Computers, like all mechanical devices, will eventually fail and data will be lost. It is only a matter of time. Knowing how and why they will fail will be very helpful if preventative measures are to be developed and the risk of data loss is to be minimized. Most users will experience data loss at one time or another. It usually only takes one data loss incident to learn the value of a backup, but unfortunately that is a lesson that is often learned the hard way. Having a secure backup is a great tool in those difficult times. A backup, however, is reactionary by its very nature. First the incident occurs and then a recovery process takes place. Avoiding the disaster in the first place is preferable. Some in safeguards and redundancies already in place can be used to create proactive measures. Table 4.2 lists the reasons for computer loss (Costas, 2002).

Table 4.2 – Reasons for Computer Loss/Data Error

Hardware or system malfunction	44%
Human error	32%
Software corruption/Program malfunction	14%
Computer viruses	7%
Natural disasters	3%

Once a disaster recovery team can identify the reasons why data loss can occur, preventive actions can be implemented. A backup of the nonprofit's data, applications, and operating systems will help the organization recover from any of the above incidents. For a number of the losses list in the table, there are preventative measures that can be implemented. The examples presented below range from expensive hardware configurations to free software updates.

- Implement Redundant Hardware
  Network hard drives can be implemented in such a way as to provide redundancy. In the event of a hardware failure, redundant equipment can safeguard the data so it may not be necessary to retrieve files from backup. Mirrored drives and drives configured in a RAID-5 configuration provide protection.
- Install Firmware and BIOS Updates
  The personal computer's or server's hardware is controlled by computer code that exists in firmware or the BIOS. Hardware manufacturers often release updates of this code to improve the efficiency of the system.
- Install Operating System Updates, Patches, and Fixes
  Operating system manufacturers such as Microsoft and Novell are constantly supplying updates to their software to correct problems and close loopholes in their operating systems. Many bugs and vulnerabilities are exploited by computer hackers. Installing updates, patches, and fixes will minimize a nonprofit's liabilities.
- Install Software Updates, Patches and Fixes, Including Anti-virus Definition Updates
  Upgrading application software such as Microsoft Office, Lotus Notes, or Adobe Acrobat can become expensive and in many instances is not truly necessary. A nonprofit also has the opportunity to download updates for free from the web.
- Run Utility Programs
  Just as an automobile requires preventative maintenance, so does a computer. Operating systems often come equipped with utility programs such as Check Disk (CHKDSK) and a disk defragmenter (DEFRAG) to maintain healthy computers. A nonprofit can run these tools during the day, lunch time, or off hours. Running them off hours helps minimize the impact on the users' work time but also allows these programs sufficient time to run.
- Lock Down Equipment
  Computer equipment is expensive. For a nominal fee, a nonprofit can install security cables to lock down the computers. Additionally, locks on server room doors and

offices work wonders. Most PCs and servers also permit the CPU cases to be secured with a lock to prevent the internal components from being stolen.

- Install and Configure an Uninterruptible Power Supply (UPS)
An Uninterruptible Power Supply (UPS) can supply power to a computer or server for a limited amount of time in the event of power loss. Files which are open or in use can become corrupt if the hosting computer is shut down improperly. The UPS won't run the equipment indefinitely, but it will allow equipment to shut down properly. This feature should be configured to run automatically in the event that a power outage occurs during off hours. APC (American Power Conversion) offers a wide array of UPSs which will meet the needs of a nonprofit. Some UPSs have the added advantage of acting as a conditioner, i.e., dealing with power surges and drops so the change in electrical current won't adversely affect sensitive computer components. Surge protectors offer this same advantage without the backup power supply. It is also of value to note that surge protectors are not the same as lightning arrestors, i.e., those devices designed to stop a lightning strike from harming equipment.

- Clean the backup tape drive
Backup tape drives require regular cleaning. Without cleaning, the drives will eventually malfunction or not properly record data.

- Make backups before upgrading
During upgrades a number of tasks could go wrong. Backing up a computer's essential files immediately before performing an upgrade alleviates the worry.

- Go looking for trouble – event logs
PCs and servers have event logs which track errors reported by software and hardware. Review the event logs periodically to determine if a computer is operating within normal parameters.

- Tighten the security policy
A good security policy will permit employees to gain access to the data they need without inhibiting them and at

the same time prevent users from accidentally or intentionally gaining access to restricted information. Reviewing and tightening the policy is a safeguard worth performing. Most good security policies start with the implementation of good passwords.

- Firewall
  More and more individuals and nonprofits are becoming permanently connected to the Internet as the cost of connecting drops. Cable modems and DSL are becoming viable connections. With these permanent connections, a nonprofit should use a firewall, even if they do not host their own website. Permanent connections not only connect a nonprofit's network to the Internet, but connects all of the "undesirables" of the Internet to the network. Hackers using probes can find open or responding IP addresses. A nonprofit should not think they will not be found.

Revenue Impact

Downtime is just as damaging to nonprofits as it is to commercial organizations, although it may not be as apparent at first glance. For-profits exist to provide goods or services to customers. For businesses, a disruption of normal activities from a disaster, whether it is to a store front, supply chain, website, or whatever, will cause customers to find other vendors because of waiting (Real, 2002). Nonprofits have income sources other than sales so many of the concerns do not necessarily apply. Nonprofits are in a slightly different category – they rely primarily on donations for their revenue. 76% of all revenue contributed to nonprofit organizations comes from individuals (AAFRC Trust for Philanthropy, 2002).

If a disaster strikes, chances are the vital communication link between a nonprofit and its donors will be hindered or stopped altogether. This may not seem terribly tragic so long as the nonprofit eventually resumes its activities, but the consequences can be quite devastating. If a nonprofit's communication and fundraising activities which targets individuals are stopped, the effects will be very harmful for several reasons. First, donors who are most likely to re-contribute to the nonprofit, i.e., those who have given to the same organization in recent history, may not do so (Rainey, 2003). The longer the time lapse of communication between a nonprofit and a donor, the more difficult it will be to renew that donor. Second, competing nonprofits will be soliciting funds and trying to acquire the donors of the disaster-stricken organization. In the absence of hearing from one organization, a donor will be much more inclined to give to another. Reacquiring those donors will be very difficult and expensive.

If a disaster should occur at a nonprofit, it will be necessary to immediately secure new revenue to counter the expenses associated with downtime and repair. Money from insurance policies may be slow in arriving and may not cover all expenses. Working with the development department of the nonprofit, a disaster recovery team should identify several resources that can be tapped in the event of a crisis. This process is not as easy as it sounds. Finding reliable sources of income for nonprofits is already challenging. Board members may be asked to make additional contributions or speak with their contacts in the hopes of driving in revenue. This, however, may not be sufficient. Grants may not be awarded in a timely fashion to meet such an urgent need. Since the public, and specifically individuals, make up the largest source of contributions, a public emergency appeal may be warranted. Building an appeal will take significant time and energy. Important to the appeal process is the list of names to whom solicitations will be sent. Identifying donors that have already contributed to the organization will be important. High dollar donors, monthly contributors, and donors with a long history of giving should be among the first to be contacted. These individuals have identified themselves, not just as regular contributors, but also as a group of people who are dedicated to the nonprofit's mission. The nonprofit may choose to target more people, but should target revenue sources rather than make blind appeals.

Vendors and Partners

A nonprofit's hands will definitely be full during the creation of a disaster recovery plan. There will be considerable time spent on research, documentation, and preventative measures. In addition to performing internal risk analyses, a nonprofit should also be concerned about its vendors and business partners. Many activities and much of the nonprofit's information such as fundraising, data processing, list management, and event planning may take place outside of the nonprofit's facility. Even though these items exist outside of the nonprofit's doors, it does not mean the nonprofit shouldn't be concerned. Nonprofits should find out if their vendors and partners have disaster recovery plans and they should investigate the depth and coverage of their plans.

Nonprofits often spend considerable time selecting vendors and other professionals with whom they partner. One of the criteria to include in proposals is some disaster recovery material. Do not just take the word of a vendor on the implementation of the plan. Ask questions and determine if the course of action is to your liking. Some questions to ask may be:

- What type of security is used at the vendor's facility?
- Is there a fire file or other backup of the data? What is the frequency with which the files are backed up?
- What level of insurance does the vendor carry?
- What risk analyses have been performed and what preventative measures/safeguards have been installed?
- Does the vendor make use of an emergency site, such as a hot/warm/cold site?

There are a number of questions to ask a vendor. While it may not be necessary to audit every aspect of the vendor's plan, it is necessary to do some preliminary investigation. The nonprofit's future is just as at stake as the vendor's.

Questions for Review and Implementation

1. What are the purposes of conducting risk analyses?
2. What key pieces of information should be identified in risk analyses?
3. What types of disasters could affect a nonprofit? What types could specifically affect your nonprofit?
4. How can a nonprofit maximize the use of its resources in disaster recovery through risk analyses?
5. What are the most likely reasons for a computer failure to occur?

6. What can be implemented in advance to prevent a computer failure?
7. What concerns may arise relating to the revenue sources of a nonprofit?
8. Why should nonprofits be concerned with the lag time available in fundraising appeals when it comes to disaster recovery?
9. What initial steps can be taken to raise revenue quickly by a nonprofit?
10. What concerns should a nonprofit have about its vendors/partners?

Chapter 5
Implementation and Updates

When did Noah build the ark? Before the flood.

A portion of a disaster recovery plan begins immediately following a disaster during the reaction phase. A significant portion of the plan, however, gets implemented before the disaster ever takes place. A successful plan will be both proactive and reactive in nature. The time of a disaster is not the time to begin implementation. The implementation of a plan exists in several steps, including:

- Get the word out
- Decide in advance who will respond to what actions
- Purchase redundant equipment
- Document the procedures and plans
- Store materials both on- and off-site
- Test the plan and schedule future tests
- Update the plan

Get the Word Out

A number of people will know about the development of the organization's plan. After all, just about every division or department should have participated in the early stages of the plan's formation, e.g., SOP development and identification of vital systems. All employees completed an information contact sheet. It is important at this stage for everyone to be informed that a formal and permanent plan exists. The disaster recovery team leader should take charge of communication with employees. People should be informed of how to respond in the event of an emergency and where to go in the event of an evacuation. Disseminating information will reduce panic which arises during these types of incidents.

Make Decisions in Advance

During critical and emergency situations people have a tendency to not think clearly. Instead they react without thinking. One of the benefits of disaster recovery planning is the ability to provide guidance in hastened events. The disaster recovery team should decide in advance who is going to perform what action during the reaction and short-term phases of recovery. By mapping out plans or steps in advance, several things can be accomplished. First, the work can be distributed among several employees. This has the benefit of not overloading one person with too much work and it will allow for multiple recovery actions to occur simultaneously, thereby reducing the nonprofits downtime. Second, the employees will be able to start the recovery process with a limited amount of supervision. Time will be of the essence and the situation will be hectic. It would not be the time to begin training individuals on the nature, sensitivity, and urgency of short-term and long-term recovery.

Clearly defining what is required of employees will greatly help them in their tasks. There are several ways of conveying this information effectively. One way is to build an ordered checklist of tasks. Another is to create decision trees outlining both the logic and the steps needed to restore operations. There may be several trees in place – each for different activities or departments. A decision tree will contain a series of logical (yes/no) questions and resulting action steps. There are some basic principles to keep in mind when designing the decision trees. The logic contained within the trees should be as simple as possible. Complicated decisions should be broken down into simpler tasks if possible. A tree should be self-

Figure 5.1 – Fire drill decision tree

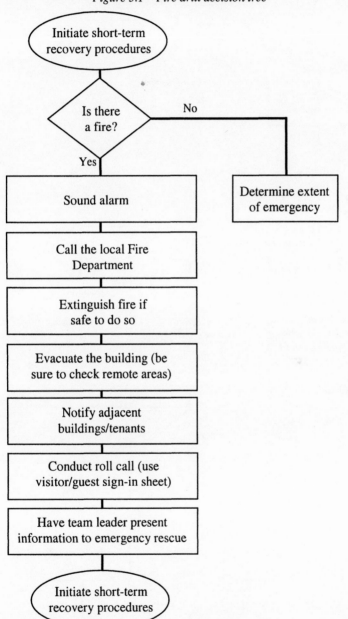

Figure 5.2 – Partial decision tree for loss of power

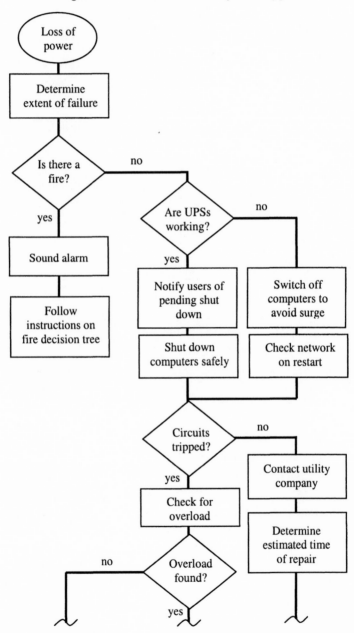

explanatory and not so involved that employees can't follow it. The alternative to complex logic is to create longer flow diagrams with simpler logic and more individual steps. Examples appear in Figures 5.1 and 5.2.

Purchase Redundant Equipment

Nonprofits often have limited financial resources. If an organization can afford it, they may want to consider purchasing redundant equipment. This equipment will be identical in model and manufacturer to existing resources. There are several advantages to acquiring this equipment. Legacy equipment (e.g., outdated or no longer manufactured) will necessitate an exact copy of the equipment to be installed on the system so software will continue to operate if damaged. Another advantage is it will reduce the amount of short-term recovery because it will not be necessary to wait for replacement products to be shipped. They will already be available and (here's the best part) they will have already been configured and tested for use with the existing infrastructure. This will require front end work to be done by the nonprofit prior to a disaster, but the concerns of configuration and compatibility will all be but eliminated. Here's an example of a good implementation of this strategy:

A nonprofit organization has a reasonably good network configuration for its employees to use. It has a backup device and is connected to the Internet. The nonprofit hosts its own web site and e-mail server. Because of this configuration, there is a firewall. The firewall is both a stand-alone and dedicated piece of equipment that exists just outside of the scope of the network to avoid users and hackers alike from circumventing it. (It wouldn't be much good if users could connect to the Internet by going around it, would it?) Because of the configuration, it is difficult to back up the firewall. The backup device does not have access to the stand alone machine. The solution chosen by this nonprofit was to purchase a redundant server and configure it to be identical to the existing firewall. In the event of system failure, the redundant firewall can be taken out of storage, dropped into place, and immediately turned on. The second firewall is already configured for the existing e-mail and web site setup. Redundant equipment greatly eases the burden during recovery.

Ideally, it would be nice to have an entire infrastructure duplicated and ready to go, if necessary. Unfortunately that is generally not feasible. Rather than unnecessarily drive up capital costs, a nonprofit could target specific systems. Using the data obtained from identifying vital, important, and useful systems as outlined in Chapter 2, a disaster recovery team can make the most of its finite resources. In the previous example, the nonprofit determined that because the organization hosts its own website and relies heavily on its e-mail server, it was necessary to ensure the connection and safety of that system. The purchasing of specific redundant equipment is driven by the current infrastructure and the value of specific components.

Document Procedures and Plans

Preparing good documentation is important to any plan. Written procedures and plans foster an institutional memory beyond any one person. It is also one of the more efficient means of passing instructions and guidelines from the disaster recovery team leader to the team, itself, and to the rest of the employees. Written instructions remove ambiguity. Not all prepared material and documentation is equal. A nonprofit's goals should be to create good, reliable material. This documentation should:

- Be understandable to employees who did not serve on the disaster recovery team. Undecipherable notes are not helpful.
- Be complete. Readers should not have to go far to find supporting information. Readers will want as few interruptions or road blocks as possible in performing the listed tasks. Having employees track down other pieces of information at this time is counter productive.
- Be assembled in a modular fashion. Updates to plans, as it will be explained later in this section, will be essential to the longevity of any plan. If documentation is assembled in blocks, it will be easy to locate information and update the data. For example, certain procedures executed during short-term and long-term recovery will require phone calls

to be made. If a nonprofit changes its business partners during the life of a plan, contact information will change as well. Procedures should provide information necessary to carry out given steps, but the contact information can be stored in one document in the appendix. It will be easier to update a single contact page, rather than be forced to update all of the procedures in a plan. Documentation has the benefit of creating a good starting point for future revisions. It is much easier to update an existing plan than it is to create a new one.

- Contain detailed information for the reaction and short-term recovery phases when time is of the essence. Long-term and resumption procedures can be more open ended to allow for employees to implement different approaches based on the results of short-term fixes.

- Lastly, documentation should be stored in an easily accessible format. While storing documentation on disks or CDs may eliminate the need for copious amounts of paper, it may not be the be the easiest of formats to access during an emergency.

Off-Site Storage

The importance of this section can't be stated enough. Disaster recovery materials need to be stored at a safe, off-site location 24 hours a day. It may seem like common sense to have these materials off-site, but many nonprofits only store a portion of their materials in a safe location. It won't matter how good a plan is if all of the materials get destroyed in a disaster. With that said, there is a need to be specific about what information is stored off-site. A number of nonprofits currently do not take enough of their documentation and related material away from their main facility/office. According to the Spring 2003 survey, 41% of those nonprofits which back up their records do not store their financial records, audits, contracts, insurance forms, and SOPs off-site. 46% do not have employee contact information off-site. Nonprofits need to ensure that the following materials are stored at a safe facility away from their main office/site:

- Backups of network information. Backups should not be stored on-site. If something catastrophic occurs at the site, a backup would be useless. It may be temporarily inconvenient to restore backed up materials from the tape if the tape is not local, but it ensures for safer data. Some nonprofits back up their computer information on a rotating set of disks or tapes, but return the tape to the facility the following morning and leave with a different tape in the evening. Essentially, the tape is only off-site during the hours of 5PM to 8AM. If an incident were to occur during normal business hours, the backups which were so meticulously transported off-site at night, would be ineffective.
- Contact Information. Emergency contact information should be both on- and off-site. The lists of names and telephone numbers need to be accessible to the disaster recovery team off-site. The employee phone tree should be available to all employees at their homes.
- Important documents. This list is lengthy and varies from nonprofit to nonprofit, but should include: three years' worth of 990s, tax exempt applications, by-laws, bank statements, audits, signed contracts, serial numbers for hardware and software, inventories, and insurance policies.
- The disaster recovery plan itself. It will be nearly impossible to remember all of the aspects and details of a thorough disaster recovery plan.
- Redundant equipment. It will be hard enough to get approval to spend money on redundant equipment. To have it damaged or unusable when it is needed most will be horrific.

In short, everything created by the disaster recovery plan will need to be stored off-site. It may take a large box, or several large boxes to get the material stored together in a quickly accessible fashion, but it will be worth it.

Deciding what materials to store off-site is one thing, but deciding where and how far away to store the materials is another matter. The general rule of thumb is to store the materials out of the proximity of the disaster and danger that caused the first incident.

Experts in the field of disaster recovery say the distance varies depending on the type of impending disaster. The range which is considered safe starts at approximately 21 miles (for minor incidents) up to 105 miles (for large incidents, such as hurricanes) (Weems, 2003). 105 miles may be inconvenient for some nonprofits and for some of the disaster materials, i.e., carting a backup tape 105 miles may be excessive. Most of the materials in the disaster recovery storage will not be needed on a routine basis. Each nonprofit will need to decide for itself what a good precaution will be.

On-Site Storage

The chief disadvantage to off-site data is its inaccessibility. Nonprofits may not be able to access files, forms, and data that have been backed up as quickly as they might like. This identifies an issue of understanding. Backups and files stored for disaster recovery purposes are not meant to serve as daily, working copies of

---

Case History:
The Value of Remote Off-Site Locations

A small company located in Maryland experienced a fire in its office in March of 2002. Whatever computer equipment was not destroyed outright by the fire was either melted by the heat of the blaze or damaged by water from fighting the fire. The backup tapes which were stored on-site directly above the computers and the tape drive itself were melted. One PC's hard drive was sent to a data recovery vendor where virtually everything was recovered. The cost of the salvage operation was $1,600 per hour. It took approximately 6 weeks for the data to be returned to the company in Maryland. A temporary office had to be established while a long-term solution was drafted.

---

the files. Employees should not be accessing them routinely. The files should be used to restore copies of working documents that have been lost and then immediately returned to storage. The danger in having employees referring to copies in storage is that files will be misplaced, lost, or not returned. A disaster recovery team may believe that certain files are secure only to find out in an untimely circumstance that employees have been raiding the files to gain access to the organized information. The alternative to off-site storage is to make use of on-site storage. The practice of on-site storage of disaster recovery material is common. Many nonprofits choose to store sensitive data on-site. 25% of respondents to the Spring 2003 survey store backup tapes on-site, and 52% make use of on-site fire proof safes or cabinets. This may not be the best practice for several reasons.

Not all on-site storage devices are created equally and many nonprofits do not know the difference. The same study which indicated that 52% of nonprofits stored material in a fire proof container also indicated that nearly three-quarters of those same respondents did not know the fire rating of their safes or cabinets. Safes and cabinets are rated by Underwriters Laboratories in terms of their thickness, theft-resistance, and ability to maintain a steady internal temperature for a short amount of time during a fire. If something catastrophic occurs at the nonprofit's site, the on-site file storage container may not adequately protect its contents. Table 5.1 lists the failure temperatures for various mediums (*Disaster Recovery Planning: Preparing for the Unthinkable*, 3/E by Toigo, Jon William, © Reprinted by permission of Pearson Education, Inc., Upper Saddle River, NJ). If a nonprofit chooses to invest in on-site storage, the nonprofit should be aware of the container's limitations and the risks associated with its use.

Table 5.1 – Temperature Limits of Mediums

Device	Temperature of Failure
Magnetic tapes and diskettes	100-125°F
Hard disks	145-149°F
Paper	350°F
Microform	225-300°F

Test the Plan

No plan is foolproof. A disaster recovery plan will be no exception. Every plan should be tested before it can be considered complete. Thorough tests will identify data gaps, response times, flaws in logic, responsiveness of employees and the strength of the disaster recovery team. A live incident is not the time to test a plan or determine if it is viable. Testing can occur on several different levels. Small tests can be conducted to test portions or specific areas in a plan and full-scale drills can be run to analyze the effectiveness of the overall plan. Plan on running both types of tests. Testing can become very unpopular as it disrupts the normal activities and routines of employees. Therefore, you must require employees to participate. There will inevitably be one or two people who are "too busy" to get off the phone and join everyone else in a fire drill. This identifies the first level of weakness in a plan: non-cooperative employees. The disaster recovery team and leader should be able to positively motivate people and encourage them – after all, the plan is for their benefit.

When to test

Tests should be both announced and unannounced. It is easy to perform your best when you know people are watching. Since the purpose of a test is not to frighten employees but rather to improve the disaster recovery plan, conduct announced drills first. During these drills employees should record glitches and pitfalls in the system as they encounter them. Armed with this information, the disaster recovery team can revise the existing plans, correct false assumptions, and improve weaknesses.

With initial tests out of the way and the kinks removed, the time to conduct tests to improve efficiency can begin. These tests can be both announced and unannounced. Determine if systems were restored within the appropriate amount of time. Be honest about identifying the weaknesses in the system and fix what needs correcting. These trial runs will prepare both employees and the disaster recovery team.

While it is a little absurd to run frequent tests – an employee revolt may ensue – it is worthwhile to perform annual or semi-annual tests. New employees will need to become acquainted

Case History:
The Value of a Test

A large nonprofit in Northern Virginia experienced a server crash in 1998. The tape backup had not been tested and it was discovered that a backup had not been performed in over one month's time. It took approximately 4 - 6 months for the staff to recreate the work stored on the server and the office was backlogged for nearly 8 months.

with procedures. As new systems, hardware, software, and procedures are implemented, they will need to be incorporated into the disaster recovery plan. In the event that any of these systems are unintentionally not incorporated, periodic tests should catch them.

What to test

The short answer on what to test is "everything." Fire drills and evacuations should be performed. Phone/communication trees should be tested. Create a test message that needs to be passed through all of the branches to determine the speed and effectiveness of the communication line. In the event that information accidentally becomes blurred, try to pinpoint what may have occurred. Not only should tape backups be run and error logs checked, but the restore procedure should also be tested. (Managers may be surprised to discover some IT personnel can run a backup procedure, but need to learn how to properly restore files.) If data is stored at an electronic vault, determine how long it will take to have data returned to the nonprofit's site. If the nonprofit makes use of a hot-site or cold-site, tests should be performed to find out how long it will take for the emergency site to become operational. A hot-site should be ready immediately. A cold-site will need time to prepare and bring all vital systems online. An additional test to conduct is the retrieval from storage the off-site disaster recovery material and the installation of redundant equipment and any necessary software. Periodically check to see how long it will take to obtain replacement equipment. Not every piece of equipment on a nonprofit's network will have redundant equipment. The purpose of this is to identify how long it will take to order and ship equipment. If reviews seem to be indicating an increasing lag time, it may be necessary to select new equipment or revisit the idea of purchasing redundant equipment. Test it all and improve the responsiveness. The more that the short-term discovery time can be decreased, the better the chances of the nonprofit's survival.

It will be easy for future tests to fall by the wayside once the initial tests are completed. Schedule the tests early. Computer calendar programs, such as Outlook, can record events years in advance. When desk calendars are replaced, make a note to transfer test dates. Multiple people should know when tests are to be performed in the event that the team leader or initiator becomes unavailable or leaves the nonprofit.

Update the System

One of the discouraging aspects of disaster recovery is that they will never be finished. The design and implementation may have been executed, but the plan will always need to be updated and improved. As nonprofits grow and expand their services, disaster recovery plans will need to be updated. Even if the nonprofit maintains its level of service, the plan will still be in need of updating. New hardware and software will need to be incorporated into the existing plan. New employees will need to be informed of procedures and added to the phone lists. As employees leave, their information should be removed from documents. As contracts get renewed and new ones formed they will need to be included as well. There will always be new information to be included in disaster recovery plans.

To avoid maintenance of the disaster recovery plan from becoming overwhelming, a number of mechanisms can be established. First, annual reviews of the existing plan can be scheduled. Second, individual departments can incorporate updates into their procedures. As new employees join the nonprofit, the human resources department can gather phone and emergency contact information. As new computer equipment is acquired, the information technology department can record serial numbers and proof of ownership material (and make sure it makes it to the insurance company's inventory). As contracts are signed, the finance department can generate copies of the signed documents. To make the plan evergreen (i.e., continually fresh or updated), responsibility needs to shared by the different departments and assigned. If tasks are not assigned, many will assume that others will pick up the slack. Implement an evergreen strategy from a plan's inception and updates will not be burdensome.

Another technique in easing the burdens of maintenance is to rotate employee placement on the disaster recovery team. Rotation has both pros and cons. While this will distribute the workload and allow more employees to take ownership of the plan, it may not always be practical to implement. Smaller nonprofits may not have the manpower. A second disadvantage is that a nonprofit may not want to have sensitive information, such as personnel files and contracts, viewed by a wider group of employees. Third, in some organizations, team rotation actually runs countercurrent to the maintenance and upkeep of a plan. New team members may feel the need to unnecessarily redo the disaster recovery plan, thereby taking the plan backwards rather than forward. Nonprofits should give this practice serious consideration before implementation.

Emergency Sites

If a nonprofit's office or facility should become damaged in a disaster to the point where employees can't work on recovery procedures, the nonprofit has the choice of waiting for repairs to be made or using an emergency site until enough repair work is done for employees to return and begin on the path to resumption. There are several different types of emergency sites that can be used and while each has its own set of characteristics, the driving principle behind their use and growing popularity is the ability to reduce the recovery time of organizations by finding a way for employees to remain functional and have access to its data. The decision to use these types of sites is up to the nonprofit. The mission of the nonprofit may dictate the need for one of these sites. For example, a nonprofit which supplies relief effort to local communities during disasters can't afford to wait for repairs and it will need to make use of a temporary emergency site to fulfill its mission. The key planning aspect to using an emergency site is to make prior arrangements with different specifications for each type of facility. The major emergency sites available to nonprofits during disaster recovery are hot sites, cold sites, and mobile sites.

Hot Site

A hot site is a business location that is ready to be used immediately upon the need for it. Everything required for the site to be fully operational has been arranged in advance. Data is synchronized on a frequent basis so it will be nearly identical to the nonprofit's data system at the time of a disaster. This set up is analogous to walking into an office with the lights and computer already on. It's not your computer or your desk, but the materials in the drawers and on the PC are yours. Web sites that can't afford to experience down-time might use a hot site.

Cold Site

A cold site is an emergency site which requires some set up before it is operational. Employees will not be able to immediately walk into a cold site and begin working as they would with a hot site. This is similar to walking into a dark warehouse. It may be a temporary place to work from, but it will require the moving of some furniture and the set up of some computer equipment before it is ready to work.

Mobile Site

A large coach, bus, RV, or tractor trailer equipped with the necessary equipment can serve as a mobile site. The primary advantage here is that the office can go to the employees rather than vice versa. This makes it convenient for nonprofits that might bring relief effort to communities by going to the "front lines." The disadvantage to mobile sites is there limited room and size.

Alternative Emergency Sites

There are alternatives to using emergency sites. Not many nonprofits will be able to afford the expense of an emergency and even fewer will be willing to expend the time and effort it will take to preplan. If a nonprofit can't afford an emergency site, they may be able to create a make shift site out of a local chapter's office, their national headquarters, a hotel conference room, or maybe even an educational facility's computer lab. While they are not traditional emergency sites, hotels, high schools, and colleges shouldn't be dismissed. Hotels have better than average Internet access and phone lines and schools, which may not be used at night, on the weekends, or over the summer months often have more than adequate computer systems and Internet connections. In a pinch, a nonprofit has a number of alternatives available if it is creative.

Where to Go From Here

In addition to actual modifications to the disaster recovery plan there are other manners of improving an existing plan. Training is available to employees on the topic of disaster recovery. As new techniques in the industry are developed, employees may wish to seek training in the implementation of those techniques. If a disaster recovery team is having trouble in certain areas of implementation, they may wish to get training or obtain the services of a consultant. There are a number of options available. Excellent sources of information and training are the Federal Emergency Management Association (FEMA) and the individual state governments which all have emergency management divisions of one form or another. Since the events of September 11, 2001 and the formation of the Department of Homeland Security, many states have seen an increase in funding of these state programs. The federal government and many of the state governments offer training and disaster recovery planning materials. Contact information for each, including web site addresses, appears in Appendix B – Disaster Recovery Planning Resources. If a nonprofit is seeking assistance, it may choose to engage the services of a consultant rather than a government institution. When choosing a consultant, it may be beneficial to obtain the services of a vendor who has experience with nonprofits. Many will be familiar with IT approaches and the options available to commercial organizations. Finding a consultant which understands the needs and circumstances surrounding nonprofits may be more advantageous.

Becoming well versed in current trends is also a great help during the development of a plan. There are a number of publications, such as the Disaster Recovery Journal and several web sites that are frequently updated with articles on the subject. A partial listing appears at the end of Appendix B. These resources can be good supplies of information, statistics, and conferences.

The creation process may take several weeks or even months depending on the resources available to a nonprofit. With all of the work involved, it is easy to become too inwardly focused and lose objectivity. To overcome this shortfall, it can be helpful to have an external auditor review the nonprofit's plan. An auditor will be able to provide an outsider's prospective and approaches that may be missed by the disaster recovery team.

Implementing a disaster recovery plan is not a small undertaking. It will be labor intensive and force team members to take a hard look at the vulnerabilities facing their particular organization and their employer, and find out it's not invincible. They'll discover issues facing nonprofits in general. A number of good things can arise from disaster recovery planning. Employees within the nonprofit and the members of the disaster recovery team will have a sense of camaraderie. The normal, day-to-day activities have a chance to become enhanced or optimized. Team members will have a chance to exercise some creativity and ownership. In addition, employees will gain a sense of relief and a sense of control. The biggest flaw in creating a plan, however, is gaining a false sense of confidence. A good plan will only be as good as those who plan it. They need to be dedicated. A disaster recovery team and its leader will need to remain always vigilant.

Questions for Review and Implementation

1. Why is it important to notify employees about the formal creation of a disaster recovery plan?
2. Why should a disaster recovery team attempt to make decisions prior an actual disaster occurrence?
3. How can a team leader pass information about decision making to employees?
4. What is the purpose of purchasing redundant equipment and what particular equipment should be purchased?
5. How should documentation be prepared?
6. What materials should be stored off-site?
7. What aspects of a disaster recovery plan should be tested? And what should be done with test results?
8. When should testing take place?
9. In what ways can a disaster recovery plan be updated?

10. What external resources are available for nonprofits who are developing disaster recovery plans?

Appendix A
Nonprofit Survey

In the Spring of 2003, an anonymous online survey was conducted of nonprofit organizations focusing on their current disaster recovery practices.

Audience
Over four hundred nonprofits were sent an e-mail requesting participation in the 38 question survey.

Results
42 nonprofit organizations from across the United States at both the national and local levels participated in the survey. The results appear on the following pages.

Disaster Recovery Plans
48% of nonprofit respondents had a disaster recovery plan in place at the time of the survey.

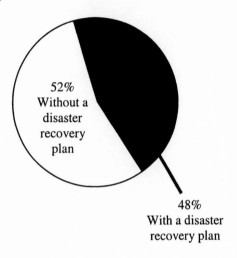

52%
Without a
disaster
recovery
plan

48%
With a disaster
recovery plan

Computer Backups
95% of nonprofit respondents back up their computer data.

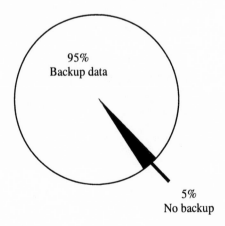

95%
Backup data

5%
No backup

Computer Backups

95% of nonprofit respondents back up their computer data.

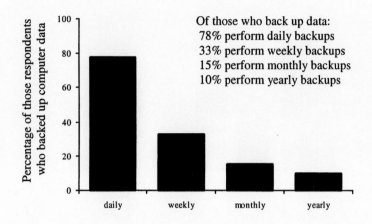

Of those who back up data:
78% perform daily backups
33% perform weekly backups
15% perform monthly backups
10% perform yearly backups

Computer Backups

95% of nonprofit respondents back up their computer data. The majority of those organizations use full backups more than other techniques.

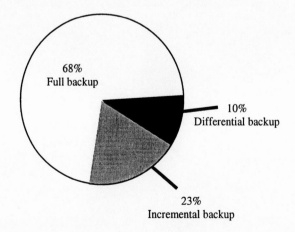

Computer Data
Not all nonprofits back up the same electronic data.

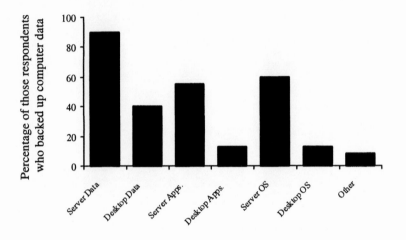

On-site/Off-site Storage
95% of nonprofit respondents make backups of electronic/computer data.

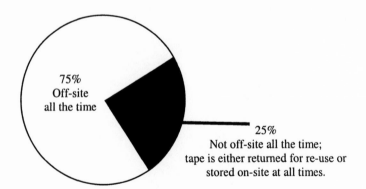

Fire-Proof Containers

Of the 52% of respondents who store on-site data in a fire-proof container, 73% do not know the fire rating of the container.

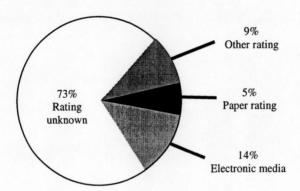

Contact Information

Of all of the charities surveyed, many collect contact information such as the home phone number of employees, who to contact in the event of an employee's accident, and emergency rescue numbers. Only 54% of charities have the information available off-site.

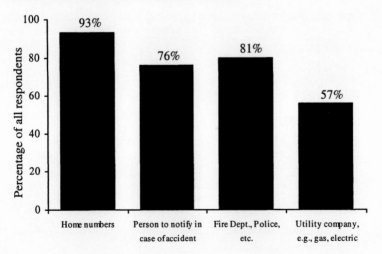

Documentation Backups

Only 69% of nonprofit respondents indicated they created backups of vital documents. Of those who backup files, a break down appears below. (Nonprofits are required to keep their tax exempt applications, supporting documents, and the last three year's worth of 990s for public inspection.)

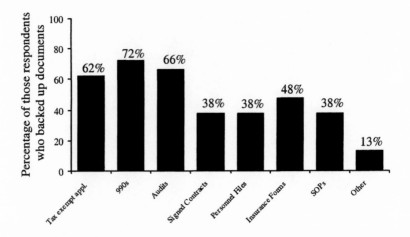

Emergency Sites

Only 24% of nonprofit respondents have an emergency site. The majority make use of mobile sites. (Several organizations have multiple emergency sites.)

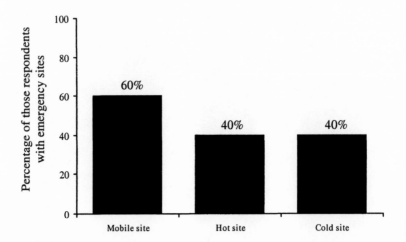

Web Sites

Of the 98% of the responding nonprofits that use web sites, very few host their own website.

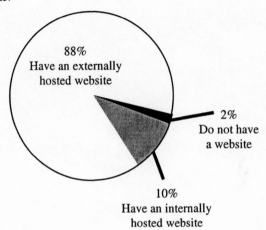

Web Sites

Of the 98% of respondents that have web sites, the majority use their site for communication and as a source of revenue, but only 27% protect their site by mirroring.

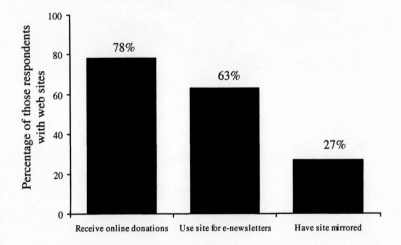

Preparedness
In most instances, it appears that those organizations with recovery plans
are better prepared to deal with a disaster.

□ = Nonprofits with disaster recovery plans
■ = Nonprofits without disaster recovery plans

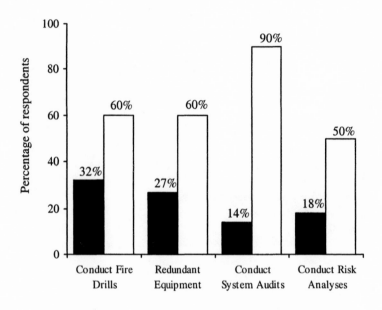

Appendix B
Disaster Recovery Planning Resources

Federal Emergency Management Agency
  500 C Street, SW
  Washington, DC 20472
  202-566-1600
  www.fema.gov
  Publications: 800-480-2520
  Training: www.training.fema.gov
  Information on volunteering or participating in the President's
  Citizen Corps: www.citizencorps.gov
  Listing of Urban Search and Rescue Teams:
  www.fema.gov/usr/usrp.shtm

National Department of Human Health Services
Office of Emergency Preparedness
  National Disaster Medical System
  12300 Twinbrook Parkway, Suite 360
  Rockville, MD 20857
  301-443-1167
  800-USA-NDMS
  ndms.dhhs.gov

National Emergency Management Association
    c/o Council of State Governments
    P.O. Box 11910
    Lexington, KY 40578
    859-244-8000
    859-244-8239
    www.nemaweb.org/index.cfm

National Fire Protection Association
    1 Batterymarch Park
    P. O. Box 9101
    Quincy, MA 02269-9101
    617-770-3000
    www.nfpa.org

U.S. Department of Homeland Security
    U.S. Department of Homeland Security
    Washington, D.C. 20528
    www.dhs.gov/dhspublic

Alabama Emergency Management Agency
    5898 County Road 41
    P. O. Box 2160
    Clanton, AL 35046
    205-280-2200
    www.aema.state.al.us

Alaska Division of Emergency Services
    P. O. Box 5750
    Fort Richardson, AK 99505-5750
    907-428-7000
    800-478-2337
    www.ak-prepared.com

Arizona Division of Emergency Management
    5636 East McDowell Road
    Phoenix, AZ 85008
    602-244-0504
    800-411-2336
    www.dem.state.az.us

Arkansas Department of Emergency Management
    P. O. Box 758
    Conway, AR 72033-0758
    501-730-9750
    www.adem.state.ar.us

California Office of Emergency Services
    Governor's Office of Emergency Services
    P.O. Box 419047
    Rancho Cordova, CA 95741-9047
    916-845-8400
    www.oes.ca.gov/Operational/OESHome.nsf

Colorado Office of Emergency Management
    15075 South Golden Road
    Golden, CO 80401-3979
    303-273-1622
    www.dlg.oem2.state.co.us/oem

Connecticut Office of Emergency Management
    Hartford Armory
    360 Broad Street
    Hartford, CT 06105
    860-566-3180
    www.mil.state.ct.us/oem.htm

Delaware Emergency Management Agency
    165 Brick Store Landing Road
    Smyrna, DE 19977
    302-659-DEMA
    877-SAY-DEMA
    www.state.de.us/dema

District of Columbia Emergency Management Agency
    John A. Wilson Building
    1350 Pennsylvania Avenue, NW
    Washington, DC 20004
    202-727-1000
    dcema.dc.gov/main.shtm

Florida Division of Emergency Management
    2555 Shumard Oak Boulevard
    Tallahassee, FL 32399-2100
    850-413-9900
    www.floridadisaster.org

Georgia Emergency Management Agency
    P.O. Box 18055
    Atlanta, GA 30316-0055
    404-635-7000
    www2.state.ga.us/GEMA

Hawaii State Civil Defense
    3949 Diamond Head Road
    Honolulu, HI 96816
    808-733-4300
    www.scd.state.hi.us

Idaho Bureau of Disaster Services
    Bureau of Disaster Services, Military Division
    4040 Guard Street, Building 600
    Boise, ID 83705-5004
    208-334-3460
    208-422-3429
    208-422-3430
    www2.state.id.us/bds

Illinois Emergency Management Agency
    Central Office
    110 East Adams
    Springfield, IL 62701
    217-782-2700
    www.state.il.us/iema

Indiana State Emergency Management Agency
    Indiana Government Center South
    302 West Washington Street, Room E-208
    Indianapolis, IN 26204
    317-232-3980
    www.in.gov/sema

Iowa Emergency Management Division
    Hoover State Office Building, Level A
    Des Moines, IA 50319
    515-281-3231
    www.state.ia.us/government/dpd/emd

Kansas Division of Emergency Management
    2800 SW Topeka Boulevard
    Topeka, KS 66611-1287
    785-274-1409
    www.accesskansas.org/kdem

Kentucky Emergency Management
    100 Minuteman Parkway
    Frankfort KY, 40601
    502-607-1682
    kyem.dma.state.ky.us

Louisiana Department of Emergency Preparedness
    7667 Independence Boulevard
    Baton Rouge, LA 70806
    225-925-7500
    www.loep.state.la.us

Maine Emergency Management Agency
    72 State House Station
    Augusta, Maine 04333
    207-626-4503
    www.state.me.us/mema

Maryland Emergency Management Agency
    State Emergency Operations Center
    5401 Rue Saint Lo Drive
    Reistertown, MD 21136
    410-517-3600
    877-MEMA-USA
    www.mema.state.md.us

Massachusetts Emergency Management Agency
    400 Worcester Road
    Framingham, MA 01702-5399
    508-820-2000
    800-982-6846
    www.mass.gov/mema

Michigan Emergency Management Division
    Michigan Department of State Police
    4000 Collins Road
    Lansing, MI 48909
    517-333-5042
    www.michigan.gov/msp

Minnesota Division of Emergency Management
    Emergency Response Commission
    444 Cedar Street, Suite 223
    Saint Paul, MN 55101-6223
    651-296-2233
    www.dps.state.mn.us/emermgt

Mississippi Emergency Management Agency
P.O Box 4501
Jackson, MS 39296-4501
1410 Riverside Drive
Jackson, MS 39202-1297
601-352-9100
www.msema.org/index.htm

Missouri – State Emergency Management Agency
P. O. Box 116
Jefferson City, MO 65102
2302 Militia Drive
Jefferson City, MO 65101
www.sema.state.mo.us/semapage.htm

Montana Disaster and Emergency Services
P.O. Box 4789
1900 Williams Street
Helena, Montana 59604-4789
406-841-3911
www.state.mt.us/dma/DES/index.shtml

Nebraska Emergency Management Agency
1300 Military Road
Lincoln, NE 68508
402-471-7421
877-297-2368
www.nebema.org

Nevada Division of Emergency Management
2525 South Carson Street
Carson City, Nevada 89701
775-687-4240
www.dem.state.nv.us

New Hampshire Office of Emergency Management
New Hampshire Department of Safety
Division of Fire Safety & Emergency Management
Office of Emergency Management
10 Hazen Drive
Concord, NH 03305
603-271-2231
www.nhoem.state.nh.us

New Jersey Office of Emergency Management
P. O. Box 7068
West Trenton, NJ 08628
609-882-2000 ext. 6050
www.state.nj.us/njoem

New Mexico Office of Emergency Services and Security
New Mexico Department of Public Safety
Office of Emergency Services and Security
P.O. Box 1628
Santa Fe, NM 87504
www.dps.nm.org/emergency

New York State Emergency Management Office
State Emergency Management Office
1220 Washington Avenue
Suite 101, Building 22
Albany, NY 12226-2251
518-457-8900
www.nysemo.state.ny.us

North Carolina Department of Crime Control & Public Safety -
Division of Emergency Management
Headquarters and Disaster Recovery Operations Center
116 West Jones Street
Raleigh, NC 27699
919-733-3737
www.dem.dcc.state.nc.us

North Dakota Emergency Management
  P. O. Box 5511
  Bismarck, ND 58506-5511
  701-328-8100
  www.state.nd.us/dem

Ohio Department of Public Safety Emergency Management Agency
  2855 West Dublin-Granville Road
  Columbus, OH 43235-2206
  614-889-7150
  www.state.oh.us/odps/division/ema

Oklahoma Department of Civil Emergency Management
  P.O. Box 53365
  Oklahoma City, OK 73152-3365
  405-521-2481
  www.odcem.state.ok.us

Oregon Emergency Management
  595 Cottage Street NE
  Salem, Oregon 97301
  503-378-2911
  www.osp.state.or.us/oem

Pennsylvania Emergency Management Agency
  Executive Office
  2605 Interstate Drive
  Harrisburg, PA 17110
  717-651-2007
  www.pema.state.pa.us

Rhode Island Emergency Management Agency
  645 New London Avenue
  Cranston, RI 02920
  401-946-9996
  www.state.ri.us/riema

South Carolina Emergency Management Division
　　1100 Fish Hatchery Road
　　West Columbia, SC 29172
　　803-737-8500
　　www.state.sc.us/emd

South Dakota Division of Emergency Management
　　500 East Capitol Avenue
　　Pierre, SD 57501-5070
　　605-773-3231
　　www.state.sd.us/military/sddem.htm

Tennessee Emergency Management Agency
　　3041 Sidco Drive
　　Nashville TN 37204
　　615-741-0001
　　www.tnema.org

Texas Division of Emergency Management
　　Emergency Management Service
　　P. O. Box 4087
　　Austin, Texas 78773-0001
　　512-424-2138
　　www.txdps.state.tx.us/dem

Utah Division of Emergency Services and Homeland Security
　　Room 1110, State Office Building
　　Salt Lake City, UT 84114
　　801-538-3400
　　800-SL-FAULT
　　cem.utah.gov

Vermont Emergency Management
　　103 South Main Street
　　Waterbury, VT 05671-2101
　　802-244-8721
　　www.dps.state.vt.us/vem

Virginia Department of Emergency Management
   Public Affairs Office
   10501 Trade Court
   Richmond, VA 23236
   804-897-6510
   www.vdem.state.va.us

Washington Military Department Emergency Management Division
   Emergency Management Division
   MS: TA-20, Building 20
   Camp Murray, WA 98430-5122
   800-562-6108
   253-512-7000
   www.wa.gov/wsem

West Virginia Office of Emergency Services
   State Capitol Complex
   Building 1, Room EB-80
   1900 Kanawha Boulevard, East
   Charleston, WV 25305-0360
   304-558-5380
   www.state.wv.us/wvoes

Wisconsin Emergency Management
   2400 Wright Street
   Madison, Wisconsin 53704
   608-242-3232
   badger.state.wi.us/agencies/dma/wem/index.htm

Wyoming Emergency Management Agency
   5500 Bishop Boulevard
   Cheyenne, WY 82009-3320
   307-777-4900
   wema.state.wy.us

BankersOnline.com
www.bankersonline.com
(Under "Banker Tools" go to the links for: Disaster Recovery Guidelines and Disaster Recovery & Business Resumption Planning)

Disaster Recovery Information Exchange
www.drie.org

Disaster Recovery Journal
11131 East South Towne Square
St. Louis, MO 63123
314-894-0276
www.drj.com

Disaster Recovery World
www.disasterrecoveryworld.com

The Disaster Resource Guide
www.disaster-resource.com

Federal Financial Institutions Examinations Council
www.ffiec.gov

Ready.gov
www.ready.gov

Rothstein Catalog on Disaster Recovery
www.rothstein.com/data/index.htm

Bibliography

AAFRC Trust for Philanthropy. (2002). *Giving USA 2002.*
Indianapolis, IN.

Costas, William. (2002) "Leading Causes in Data Loss." Data-Protectors.com. May 1, 2003. http://www.data-protectors.com.

Maiwald Eric and William Sieglein. (2002) *Security Planning and Disaster Recovery.* McGraw-Hill/Osborne. Berkeley, CA. p 232.

Margeson, Bill. (2003) "The Human Side of Data Loss." *Disaster Recovery Journal.* Vol. 16, No. 2. p 48.

New Jersey Division of Archives and Records Management. *Vital Records Management.* http://www.state.nj.us/state/darm

Pelant, Barney. (2003) "Probability or Consequence." *Disaster Recovery Journal.* Vol. 16. No. 1. pp. 28-29.

Rainey, Pat of National Fundraising Lists. Interview. May 16, 2003.

Real, Frank J. (2002) "Time Is Money When Recovery Lost Data." *Disaster Recovery Journal.* Vol. 15. No. 4. pp 14-16.

Tagger, Oded. (2002) "Disaster recovery planning issues - part 1." March 27, 2002. Issue 12. http://www.mainframeweek.com

Toigo, Jon W. (2002) *Disaster Recovery Planning: Preparing for the Unthinkable*. Third Edition. Prentice Hall, Upper Saddle River, NJ.

Turner, Dana. (2002) "Disaster Recovery Manual." Security Education Systems. May 1, 2003. http://www.nvo.com/ses.

Robinson, Michael K. (2003) "Disaster Recovery: Will Your Nonprofit Be Ready?" *2003 Washington Nonprofit Conference*. February 27, 2003.

Weems, Thomas L. (2003) "How Far is 'Far Enough?'" <u>*Disaster Recovery Journal*</u>. Vol. 16, No. 2. pp 22-28.

About the Author

Michael Robinson currently serves as the IT Director for Creative Direct Response, Inc. (CDR). CDR is a direct response fundraiser that works exclusively with national nonprofit organizations. In addition to professional fundraising services, CDR also provides training and education in such areas as disaster recovery planning for nonprofits – another means of ensuring the long lasting presence of charities.

Michael earned a BS in Chemical Engineering from Drexel University in 1994, where he simultaneously worked as a co-op and consultant for four years at Arco Chemical Company. In the Environmental, Health, and Safety division, he assisted in the development and conversion of a multi-lingual, multi-format Material Safety Data Sheet database, which earned him the company's Excel Award. After his undergraduate work, Michael studied graduate philosophy and theology with the Oblates of St. Francis de Sales. During his five-year stay with the Oblates, Michael taught science and advanced mathematics at the high school level for two years in Northern Virginia, where he earned a *Who's Who Among American Teachers* award.

Also during his time with the Oblates, Michael worked with a variety of nonprofits including serving on the board of directors for a soup kitchen in Washington, DC.

Michael then moved from the Oblates to working with the National Federation of Nonprofits. In the fall of 1999, he began working with CDR. His primary responsibilities with CDR include managing the work of the IT department, disaster recovery planning and implementation, network management, intranet development and maintenance, on-site training, new technology integration, web and FTP site support, proposal development, and *ad hoc* research. He also serves as an instructor for CDR's training seminars.

Rounding out Michael's credentials are an academic certificate in network management from Anne Arundel Community College and a number of computer certifications, including MCSA, Network+, and *i*-Net+. He is also a certified Microsoft® Office® instructor. He has nearly a dozen articles to his credit, mostly on the topics of effective use of Internet technology by charitable organizations and disaster recovery planning. Michael has prepared and delivered a number of presentations at nonprofit industry conferences.

In addition to his role as IT Director at CDR, Michael is an adjunct instructor at Anne Arundel Community College in the School of Business, Computing and Technical Studies. He teaches several courses on information technology. The courses contain a mix of both theory and practical matters.

Michael is presently a master's degree candidate in Information Technology at the University of Maryland.

Index